KIDS ON THE STREET

CARL R. RESENER & JUDY HALL

BROADMAN PRESS
NASHVILLE, TENNESSEE

© Copyright 1992 • Broadman Press
All rights reserved
4250-91
ISBN: 0-8054-5091-2
Dewey Decimal Classification: 362.7
Subject Heading: HOMELESS PEOPLE // RUNAWAY YOUTH
Library of Congress Catalog Card Number: 91-22322
Printed in the United States of America

Library of Congress Cataloging-in-Publication Data

Resener, Carl R., 1929-
    Kids on the street / Carl R. Resener and Judy Hall.
        p.   cm.
    Includes bibliographical references.
    ISBN 0-8054-5091-2
    1. Homeless children—United States.   2. Runaway children—United States.   3. Social work with the homeless—United States.   4. Church work with the homeless—United States.   I. Hall, Judy A.
II. Title.
HV4505.R473   1992
362.7′4—dc20   91-22322
                                                                    CIP

DEDICATION

This book is dedicated to the homes
across the world where a lighted candle
sits in the window. May the light never falter.

—Carl R. Resener

◆ ◆ ◆

To the thousands of volunteers
and social workers who toil endless
hours to alleviate the pain and despair
of the homeless, I dedicate this book.

—Judy Hall

89873

Preface

Four-year-old Danny was a symbol of literally thousands of homeless children and youth across America, "America the Beautiful," America, "the land of the free and the home of the brave"—yet America with perhaps one and a half million homeless youngsters on the street.

He was typical of thousands I had worked with as a teacher and as an executive with Travelers Aid and with the National Association of Social Workers, Inc. I felt that no one but a heartless beast could ignore the tousled little fellow. His deep brown eyes pierced straight into my heart, and I wanted to throw my arms around him and assure him and his mother, "Everything's gonna be all right" . . . but I couldn't.

Danny Boy, his Mickey Mouse T-shirt stained with spaghetti sauce and being restained by the dripping popsicle in his hand, was pressed close against his mother and his older brothers and sisters. Yes, his hair was shaggy, and his undernourished little body was grimy. His eyes, emblematic of the world's homeless, starving children, seemed too old for a mere slip of a child. Those eyes spoke of gnawing hunger and hurt, of uncertainty and fear.

As I stooped down to catch one of the orange droplets before it splashed on Mickey's left ear, I asked Danny, "Dear, where do you live?"

He shyly replied, "I used to live in Texas." Then, with a shrug of resignation, he added, "Now I just live in a shelter. We ain't got no home."

With mist in my eyes I visualized my own little blond grandson almost Danny's age and size. My grandson's vocabulary does not include the word "shelter." I blinked back the tears.

—Judy Hall

Maybe we can employ our experience, as well as professional knowledge, to help extinguish conflagrations in the home that fuel the flames of family adversity and breakups.

Added to all of the above is the reality that even thousands of loving, caring families are forced onto the streets because of ill health, the loss of work, or other debilitating factors.

Our overarching aim is not only to delineate the problem but hopefully to offer concrete approaches and solutions to the plight of children and youth who are displaced and misplaced. Maybe this work will help prevent future young people from becoming victims and finding themselves without a home. How? It is our hope that we can assist the reader in recognizing children as priceless gifts from the Almighty.

—*Carl R. Resener*
Judy Hall

Contents

Shooting Back, Inc.

1

Homeless Kids—An Epidemic

Only seventeen, but with the face and body that looked a decade older, Kim leaned against the wall of a typical abandoned building. She felt a kinship to objects or animals or people who were abandoned. The obscene grafitti splashed on the wall was no more obscene than her emotions, what few emotions remained.

Dear God, her dope-hazed brain thought, *How did I get here, and why am I here? If I don't turn two or three tricks, Franky will just about kill me. Maybe it'd be better if he did go ahead and do just that. I can't stand it anymore. Sometimes I want to live. Today I'd just as soon die.*

In rapid succession, she reeled off three four-letter words. She wasn't sure whether she was talking to herself or God. Since running away from home in a conventional Midwest town, she had seldom referred to God except in expletives.

Kim shook her head and spoke to the pavement, "This' not Kim. Oh, no. This' somebody else. Kim, who was going to be a movie star, Kim who was going to make it big. Whoever you are, you're not Kim anymore. You're just a piece of trash men—and even women— dump on."

Her soliloquy was interrupted by a gruff bass voice. "Hey, Baby, what about the good times with Daddy?"

· · · · · ·

Eight-year-old Jimmy had this constant pain in his "tum tum." With his alcoholic mother, he was sleeping under bridges, once in a while in a skidrow "flophouse," but most of the time out on the street.

They hadn't eaten a meal since they visited the rescue mission. In the last three days Jimmy had eaten four— or was it three?—stale soda crackers they found in a garbage can.

Like most kids his age he had fantasies and carried on conversations with himself. *It's bad that Mom can't get well. And when I say I'm hungry, she gets mad and slaps me. Right in the face. That hurts so bad.*

I don't know where we'll be tonight. I never do, and it's getting so cold. Even though I'm with Mom a lot of times, I'm awful scared.

"Mom, please, I'm so hungry!"

· · · · · ·

Susie was bone tired from walking the streets all day long. She mused to herself, *This' dumb, but I'm so worn out I can't sleep. Are Mom and Dad going to live like this for the rest of our lives? Here we are, seven of us, sleeping in this rotten old car.*

How come my folks can't get work? I don't know. They try and try, but nothing happens. It's the same old thing. The car won't run. Even if it did, we don't have any money for gas. Everytime a job comes up, they don't have a way to get there.

Her sister Rosie turned over and elbowed Susie even more awake. Mother and father are on the front seat with the baby, Jodie; and Susie, Rosie, Toby, and Josie are scrunched together in the back.

I know Mom and Dad love us. They show it. They tell us they love us every day. They want to do better, but I'm afraid the way it's going, some of us kids might even be taken away by the welfare department. A couple of workers have talked with Mom and Dad about our bad conditions. I'm just thirteen, so nobody will hire me. Maybe when I'm fourteen or fifteen, I can help bring in some money—maybe work at a fast-food place.

I know one thing for sure. I'm going to amount to something. I'll show 'em. I'm going to be a somebody, and life's going to be better. I just know . . . Zzzzz . . .

. . . . . .

"You little low life. I've had it up to here with you. I've told you ten thousand times to do what I say do, not what I do. Now I want you to get the _____ out of this house. And I don't want to see your _____ face again! You hear?

"I'll give you just long enough to pack a bag and then scram. You'll end up in prison, so I'll help move you in that direction. I ought to murderlize you, scum."

Robert (Bob) couldn't believe those words. His dad had come unglued, and he meant it. "But, Dad," Robert protested, only to be pummeled by his own flesh and blood's fists.

"Please, please, Dad, you can't mean this. I'll try to do better. Give me another chance, please!"

"No, you so and so. Out and out now. Walk out that door and don't come back!"

Within minutes Robert walked out the door. He never came back, a "throwaway kid."

His entire life was compressed into the backpack he carried. Nausea and sheer fright gnawed at the pit of his stomach. Tears were uncharacteristic of Robert, but they gushed from his eyes as he stuck out his thumb on the Interstate.

These incidents are repeated thousands of times a day in our nation and around the world. This book quite frankly is not intended as "an easy read." Neither is it sensationalized to place heavy emphasis on a subject with which numerous books and motion pictures have dealt—sex as it is related to kids on the street.

The dilemma of homeless youth and children is absolutely staggering. In spite of exposure by the media, the "average middle-class American" (if there really is one)—and if he has even a scintilla of conscience—will gasp at the immensity of this pervasive social and spiritual cancer.

Hall

You see them every day on the streets of downtown Washington, D.C., where I work—homeless men, women, and children, carrying all their worldly possessions in plastic bags, blankets, or supermarket shopping carts. Whether young or old, they are usually dirty, unkempt, smelly, and frequently talking to hallucinated companions or to no one in particular. The nation's capital has so many of these homeless people that each must "stake out" a particular territory—a street corner, park bench, or covered entrance to an office building as a daytime home. Their worn faces, all looking old (even the young ones), become so familiar you can almost forget they exist. They have become part and parcel of the everyday scenery in urban life.

The downtown office workers confront these homeless persons daily. Sometimes at least one out of three is a child or youth. These people are what the worker envisions when he or she thinks of the homeless. Why, homeless people near the White House have become a "tourist attraction," along with the Smithsonian Institution and the Washington Monument. Camera-toting families from all over the world are photographing one of the fastest-growing phenomena in the nation.

Over in the northeast part of D.C., away from the corporate business center, you can find an even faster-growing population—homeless families with children. Rarely do you see homeless children and their parents at the Metro entrances or in doorways of office complexes. But they are to be found everywhere today from large cities to small towns all over this land, even across the world.

The U.S. Department of Health and Human Services (HHS) estimates that up to one million children in the U.S. run away from home each year:

- 57 percent were from divorced parents.
- 16 percent never knew their fathers.
- 25 percent had been in mental hospitals.
- 48 percent had attempted suicide at least once.
- 40 percent are fifteen and under.

A high percentage of teen prostitutes may be termed "throwaways," that is, many have been literally cast off by their families onto the streets. Others have been kidnapped into "white slavery." Another subset of runaways is that group whose pictures and sad requests for information about them appear on milk cartons and leaflets.

Children in the Streets—Without Parents

Resener

It is estimated that nearly one million young people run away from their homes each year. Over half end up living in the streets of our cities. They have been labeled "America's lost tribe" and "children of the night."

They are also called "America's throwaways." It matters not what label one applies to street children; labels merely draw attention to a deplorable situation but offer little to the solution, if any, about how to rescue them from the streets and place them into an appropriate home situation.

It has always been difficult to keep young people at home. In fact, it is expected that youth will leave home in order to create homes of their own. Leaving home is a part of the natural process of life. A young person often leaves home to enter college, move to another town to obtain a job, or because of an adventurous spirit. In situations like these there is a continuation of "home ties and feelings." The parents reluctantly give up their authority and domination over the young person, realizing that the inner urgencies of the young will not be suppressed by the parents' fear and concern for their welfare.

In most situations, leaving home under these circumstances, though heartbreaking for the parents, is healthy for the young person in that he or she enters into adulthood with self-reliance that can only create inner strength that will establish qualities of adulthood. In most situations, being away from home eventually deepens one's feeling about home and will lead one to establish his or her home in direct relationship to character and priorities of the home he or she was privileged to have. However, in the cases of those who left home for reasons of neglect, abuse, and so forth, there is a completely different outlook as well as outcome. There is a vast difference in attitude and affection towards home for those who have been "kicked out" or run away, compared to the home where one leaves with hugs, kisses, and weighed down with candy, jams, and a box of stationery with "stamped envelopes."

The Anatomy of Running Away

When I was approached by the editors of Broadman to co-author a book on kids on the streets, I was somewhat reluctant. It was not because of a lack of knowledge. My years at the Nashville Union Mission brought me into constant contact with vast numbers of kids on the streets. Literally we have kids running in and out of all the buildings of the mission, some with parents and many without. *My reluctance came from the fact that I myself am a runaway, a foster kid.* My runaway experience did not push me to the streets like the kids we will read about. I did not become involved with drugs, sex, cults, and the like as many runaways do today. Although my experience was rather mild compared to other kids who left their homes by choice, I am aware of the hour of decision every kid goes through that ultimately leads to departure from his home and family.

My decision to run away was not created by so-called abuse, or even an adventurous spirit, but of the feeling of neglect and being unwanted. It seemed to me that I was merely "in the way." Being one of eight children, I felt that leaving would resolve many problems I had personally about where I fit in with the rest of my family.

Streets Better Than Home

There are an estimated 1.2 million homeless teens in America. No one knows for sure just how many Toms,

Dicks, and Marys are living outside of the atmosphere of home. It is difficult to count a population of teens that sleeps under bridges and on rooftops, or sometimes doesn't sleep at all, but just keeps moving from city to city. They come from all walks of life—cities, neighborhoods, farms. Their stories are many, but there is one major theme in all of their shocking, despairing stories: Life on the streets is better than life at home. Home, if it existed, included physical, emotional, or sexual abuse. More often than not, home supplied all three.[1]

Running away begins before the actual departure. The results of running away is what we hear the most about. However, the real story develops when the potential runaway's mind is developing the reasons that will cause his/her departure from the family. The buildup to the act of running away is common to all runaways, regardless of the family circumstances. There is the feeling of being an outsider, that one is different from the rest of the family. Although my brothers and sisters gave me no just cause to leave home, I still felt I did not belong. I had the feeling that matters were not going to improve.

The runaway risks that he can improve his lot by moving into a new area. He has the "greener-pastures" syndrome. I was convinced that all of us would be better off.

There is the sense of *urgency*. When I left, I had added up all the reasons why I should leave, and it seemed as if it was "now or never." Unlike some runaways, I told my dad that I wanted to move in with a family that was moving to another part of the city. I thought I would be happier living with this other couple. Since he was convinced I had made up my mind, he consented to my departure. I was nearly ten years old when I left, and it seemed if I did not make the break then, I would never have enough nerve to face Dad again. I am sure if Dad had denied my request to leave I would have left anyway.

There is the feeling of *relief*. I remember walking out the front door, believing I had resolved all of my problems. I thought, *How easy it is to replace one family for another*. Little did I know that I would have many second thoughts later on, but for the time being I thought the door of life had opened up for me. I had no desire to return.

There is the feeling of *nostalgia*. Charles Swindoll defines nostalgia as "the abnormal yearning within us to step into the time table and recover the irrevocable, that wistful dream, that sentimental journey, taken within the mind, always traveled along and therefore seldom discussed."

Runaways are not heroes, taking their lives into their own hands. Neither are they cowards, unwilling to cope with the rest of the family. I felt good and bad at the same time. I thought of the adventures I was heading for but also of what I was leaving at home. There were times when I felt I had misjudged my home and that my leaving was a condemnation that my parents perhaps did not deserve. It was a mixed-up situation. I wasn't kicked out, but at the same time, my parents didn't plead for me to stay. Many runaways on the streets today are hurting terribly inside because of their decision that led to their running away. They walk alone, talk words of encouragement to themselves, convincing themselves that they made the right choice. They sometimes wish that leaving would never have crossed their minds. It is now fifty years since I left, and one would think that years of maturity would resolve the dilemmas a boy had with his family, but I am afraid they have not. Though I have had associations with my birth family, they have always been as a "visitor," one who had been away and who would soon go away again. I have been grateful for all the times my family has made room for me when I appeared at their doorstep. I am quite sure they never realized there were times when I wanted to come in and stay.

> There are more than a million of them on the streets of our major cities, and most of us would like to believe that they are all other people's kids. They are America's lost tribe of teenage runaways, hustling boldly in doorways or retreating into distant drugged reveries. They are prostitutes, male and female, thieves petty and grand. Most act like hard cases, posing as predators so they will appear less like prey. But today, for every annual wave of new runaways, the posturing becomes an increasingly deadly game. Selling sex was always a wrenching act of forfeiting self-esteem. In the age of AIDS, prostitution is synonymous with slow suicide. And because almost all street drug users share needles, the purveyors in the doorways and alleys are also peddling wholesale death.[2]

Last year more than 30,000 Florida children between ages 10 and 17 either ran away from home or were thrown out by their parents or guardians.

Florida, of course, is not the only state with a serious problem of homeless children. As our society rapidly changes and the influences of the nuclear family continue to erode, every state is facing a crisis. Our teenagers are growing up without the structure of family, school, and church that we older adults took for granted during our formative years. The problems of adolescence are likely to overwhelm children even in the best of circumstances. But American teenagers today are running away, abusing drugs, dropping out of school, having babies and killing themselves in alarming numbers (Batchelor, 1989).

The Four Horsemen of the Apocalypse

Four main indicators of juvenile crime are:
• Child abuse
• School dropout rates
• Teenage unemployment
• Drugs and alcohol abuse

Troubled Children

According to *Home Life:*

> It is conservatively estimated that one million children will run away from home this year. Most of them will be gone only temporarily, but some will leave for an extended time and a few will never return home. The largest percentage of them are females and their average age is slightly less than 14 years.[3]

Multitudes of young people are having a difficult time establishing for themselves a place in the so-called "American dream." The following statistics reveal some of the difficulties challenging the future of every young person in America *in one day:*

• 2,753 teenagers get pregnant.
• 1,099 teenagers have abortions.
• 367 teens miscarry.
• 1,287 teenagers give birth.
• Nine children die from gunshot wounds.
• Five teenagers commit suicide.
• 609 teenagers contract gonorrhea or syphilis.

- 988 children are abused.
- 49,322 children are in public juvenile correction facilities.
- 2,269 illegitimate children are born.
- 2,989 see their parents divorce.
- 3,288 children run away from home.[4]

These statistics, as shocking as they are, hardly scratch the surface of life within our generation of young people. They do, however, reveal that there is pernicious evil in society to the extent that children live in instability. For many kids the answer is suicide or leaving home—or as many would express it: "Suicide and running to the streets are the same!"

Children Homeless with Adults

Hall

The Porter Family

"Jim, what are we gonna do?" asked Louise. "We can't stay here anymore. I just don't know how we're gonna pay the rent!" Her anxious eyes questioned her husband who had just quit his job. Even when Jim Porter was working as a cook in an Alabama city, his paycheck barely stretched enough to provide for the family. There was fifteen-year-old Anna who had been born six months after sixteen-year-old Louise had married seventeen-year-old Jim. Within five years the couple had four more children, the ten-year-old now living with Jim's mother in Texas. Then, two years ago, when the family was becoming settled in this city, little Jim, Jr., was born. Even now, Louise was two months pregnant.

Even when Jim was working, Louise worried about making ends meet. The apartment they had rented, the

only affordable one they could find and which would allow a family with so many children, was in the worst
possible part of town. Sometimes at night, the family
could hear gunfire exchanged between warring drug
dealers. Prostitution was common on the streets outside
the apartment. On more than one occasion, the children
had witnessed violence in the hallway outside their
door. Because of his job, Jim wasn't at home much, and
Louise was afraid to leave the house, especially after
dinner. She tried to keep the children close to her to protect them. If she heard or saw something which frightened her, she would even keep them home from school.
The school, struggling to educate children in such an
environment, did not have the resources to question situations where the children missed many days. So, the
Porter children were far behind their peers in school.
Over the past year, paramedics had treated several
neighborhood residents for everything from broken
bones to beatings to gunshot wounds.

The family's ability to cope finally met its match
when Jim was attacked and seriously beaten in the
apartment's side yard. Because they had no medical insurance, the Porters squeaked by with outpatient treatment for Jim at the hospital emergency room. But, that
was the last straw. They had to get out of there. So Jim
quit his job, agreeing with Louise that they had to find
another place to live and work so the family could have
decent, safe housing.

Like so many other decisions the Porters had made,
this one was made on short notice, without much con-
sideration of alternatives. Once Jim had quit his job,
the couple began to realize they didn't have the foggiest
notion of what to do next! They finally decided to go to
Louise's mother's. She could help them, and they could

see Jennifer, their ten-year-old. Like so many other families with a problem, the Porters went to a place and to people they knew.

Growing up, Louise had lived with her parents and grandparents in a small West Texas town. The family lived a hand-to-mouth existence, her father doing shift work at a small factory with frequent layoffs. Louise had six brothers and sisters, all of whom dropped out of school as soon as they were able to find work and be out on their own. When Louise became pregnant while in high school, her mother insisted that she and Jim marry immediately. It wouldn't do for the family to be disgraced. Although Louise and her mother were never close, Louise wanted to marry Jim and have her own home. Now, things weren't working out as she had dreamed they would.

When the Porters returned to their hometown, they moved in with Jim's mother, the four children still left in the home including Jennifer, their own ten-year-old. It was hard for Louise to hear her daughter call her mother-in-law "Mama." The five-room house Jim's mother had was hardly big enough for ten people. As summer grew hotter, so did the tempers of the family under these crowded conditions. And to make matters worse, Jim couldn't find any work in this town. His limited skills simply weren't needed here.

As the days stretched on, Louise and her mother-in-law began to argue about the discipline of the children. The Porter children were rowdy and boisterous, all of which was unacceptable to Jim's mother. She began to correct the children in front of Louise and Jim, implying that they were not strict enough. She made Louise feel that she was not a good mother. Why, if she were, why was Jennifer living with her grandmother instead of her parents? Stress was affecting the entire family. Jim and Louise began to argue about his mother and his inability to locate work. Louise was now four months pregnant and had had no prenatal care.

"Why don't you head north," Jim's brother Ed suggested, "and give Mom a rest? There's too many of you in that house!"

Head north was exactly what the Porters did. They moved to Minneapolis where Jim thought he could find work. This time, because they knew no one in the city, they entered a Salvation Army shelter at first. Meanwhile, helped by social workers in the local Travelers Aid, the family applied for food stamps and subsidized public housing. Jim found a job as an apprentice chef at a local hospital. For the first time in months, the family had medical insurance. Louise saw a doctor about her pregnancy.

After nearly a month in an emergency shelter, the family has been able to get into transitional housing where they can stay while they save enough money to enter public housing. Fortunately, there are some public housing units available in the near future. The children are back in school, but this time they are even further behind. It will require considerable time—even if the family is able to move into a stable living situation—for the children to catch up, both academically and emotionally. Throughout all of this, Jim and Louise, even though their relationship has been troubled, have remained together. They want to stay together for their children and for themselves. This family has not solved all its problems, but it is on its way!

Many homeless children are with one or more adults who are parents, relatives, or guardians with responsibility for their care. These are the children who are living in cars, tents, under viaducts, in shelters, or wherever their adult caretakers can scrounge up a place to stay. We use the term "adult caretakers" because some of the children are not with their biological parents but with other adults—stepparents, other relatives, or unrelated adults who have assumed responsibility for their care.

As more and more of the homeless are adults with children, the question is posed: Why are these families homeless? All over the country there are groups trying to answer this question. For example, in Texas a study in the mid-80s found that homelessness was most often caused by poverty and unemployment, followed by deinstitutionalization of the mentally ill, the lack of low-cost housing, and the reduction of federal programs. Other parts of the country have found similar results. Unemployment or underemployment and not being able to find affordable housing seem to be the most often-cited reasons for individuals and families being homeless.

A typical scenario for a family's homelessness might go like this: A two-parent family earns barely enough income to cover basic expenses. If the mother is also working, she may not have the education or skills to earn much more than enough to cover the rest of the basics or some minimal extras after the cost of child care.

The family is able to save very little, if anything, after paying for life's necessities. If an adversity happens to upset their life such as a layoff, an illness, a rent increase, or any other economic problem, the family simply has no "cushion" to help them make it through. Help from extended family or friends may be enough if the problem is short-lived. But, if the problem continues, family and friends may not be able to see the family through. This, then, is a typical situation of the awesome possibility of homelessness.

Other scenarios that can result in homelessness include family violence, marital troubles which lead to separation, drug or alcohol abuse, and the like.

The Children Left Behind

In trying to understand homelessness and its effects on children, we usually concentrate on those who are with homeless adults. We learn about children who have been living in automobiles for weeks at a time or who are subsisting in overcrowded shelters in a single room with their brothers and sisters or in one large room with only a cot or mat to call home. It is common to think about the vast numbers of single-individual adult men and women as just that—single adults. Only when we begin to talk with them do we learn that many of them are parents, only that in this case their children are living somewhere else. How many children have been "left behind"? The answer to that question is even more difficult than determining the total number of homeless children.

There are a variety of reasons why children would not be with their homeless parent(s). In a monograph entitled "Homeless Children and Their Families: A Preliminary Study," Judy Hall and Penny Maza asked both homeless individuals and homeless families about their children, those with them and those elsewhere. The results were startling! In this study, for every ten homeless adults, there were eight children affected by their homelessness, either by traveling with them or by being left behind without parental contact.[5]

Where Were the Children Left Behind?

What happened to the children who were left behind when their parent(s) has (have) become homeless? Most were with the other parent. Divorce frequently separates children from at least one parent. When the noncustodial parent becomes homeless, the separation is even more complete. The homeless parent may not be able to remain in the same community with the children and, therefore, loses contact with them.

The reasons that parent has become homeless are also reasons that interfere with his/her having contact with his/her child. For example, the alcoholic or drug-abusing parent may lose interest in his or her children or be so incapacitated that the custodial parent will not permit contact. These kinds of problems are so complex that there is no simple scenario for us to describe which will be "typical" of what is really happening in epidemic proportions.

The unemployed parent cannot provide for himself (or herself), much less provide child support for the children. The lack of support can then become a source of conflict between the parents, which can result in the custodial parent's denying access to the children to the noncustodial parent. Handling visits with the children can be complicated enough when the parent has a place to house the children. When no such place exists or is not an appropriate dwelling for children, the tendency not to visit at all is reinforced. Single homeless men have reported not having seen their children in years.

Deinstitutionalized mentally ill parents also may not have seen their children for years. In fact, they may not be able to report how many children they have or know where those children are. Even in today's so-called "enlightened" society, many people still think of mental illness as a malady the individual has brought on himself and is a quirk to be ashamed of. So, to protect the children, the extended family or the custodial parent may avoid contact with the mentally ill parent.

Having lost contact with their children is not uncommon for the alcoholic or other substance abuser as well. The problems which result from any form of substance abuse create enormous pressures on families. When these problems cause family breakup, the children are affected both before, as well as after, the breakup. When the substance abuser becomes homeless, continued contact with the children is even less likely.

> Fred looks like a wino. He is dirty, with bloodshot, watery eyes, and a two-day stubble of beard showing a lot of gray hairs. He sometimes rambles in his speech, and it takes some effort to follow his thoughts. But at times, Fred can talk almost eloquently about his "little girls, Kristie and Laura." Somehow you can almost picture them at six and seven. But then you realize that Fred hasn't seen his daughters in fifteen years! The little girls in his mind are now young adult women who haven't seen Daddy since they were very young. You wonder what they think about Daddy and why he wasn't there for them as they grew up. You hope that they had someone there who acted in the role of Daddy for them when they needed him.

Poverty and its impact on families is a story that can never be adequately covered. The stress that poverty exerts on families leads to many other problems, including child neglect and abuse. As a result, many children of poor and homeless individuals are placed in foster care. About 3 percent of the children who were left behind by their homeless parents (in the Hall and Maza study) were put into foster care. The old story of which came first, the poverty/homelessness or the abuse, cannot be determined. Actually, while their mother is homeless, the children cannot be returned to her. She, in turn, cannot qualify for AFDC benefits to support her children while her children are not with her. Without those benefits she may not be able to support her children, even if she is working. It's a vicious cycle for some parents who have left their children behind.

2

The Plight of Homeless Kids

Hall

Life on the Streets:
Physical Effects on Children

Living on the streets devastates the people out there. When they are children, the problems are intensified. Children are at critical developmental stages in their lives, both physically and emotionally. Living on the streets interrupts the normal progress of growing up. We have learned that trauma of any kind has the capacity to delay the normal progress of growing up. Living on the streets is a shock which undermines children in every aspect of their lives.

Reports on the situation of New York's homeless children (Kurtz, 1989) identified a frightening situation for the children's health. Almost half of the children had not had their immunizations, and about 10 percent of those seen by the Health Project's mobile medical unit were referred to hospitals. They were brought to the unit by their parents for acute or chronic illnesses such as anemia, pneumonia, ear infections, respiratory ailments, stomach problems, lead poisoning, hearing loss, and heart murmurs.

Doctors treating the New York homeless children ex-

Shooting Back, Inc.

pressed dismay at the extent to which these children lacked the most basic health care. The doctor responsible for the medical van, Dr. Irwin Redlener, indicated he felt the mothers, who had become homeless and were out of their familiar settings, became almost immobilized with regard to health care for their children.

Being homeless and pregnant is extremely difficult on mothers, and it can be fatal for the developing fetus. In New York City the infant mortality rate for babies born in shelters or welfare hotels is high, even higher than that of Trinidad and Tobago!

Many homeless children are under age five. Living under such conditions is particularly hard on infants. They are vulnerable to lack of proper health care and lack of food, or spoiled food because of a lack of refrigeration. And they are more vulnerable to the effects of lead poisoning.

Homeless Infants

January 1988 witnessed the deaths of two infants within a week of each other at Capitol City Inn shelter in Washington, D.C. Both babies were under the age of one year. The investigations into the cause of the deaths centered around the possibilities of foul play on the part of the parents and concerns over the spread of a disease inside the shelter. Fear and panic ran rampant among pregnant women and mothers of infants and toddlers.

One week after the death of the second child, the District of Columbia's medical examiners linked the cause of the deaths to the number of people living in the same room—in some cases, one room is shared by two to nine people. Because of the shelter's overcrowded living conditions, the infants' underdeveloped immune systems could not fight off the normal infections that result from the overcrowding of people and the lack of proper air circulation.

Losing one's home is so chaotic it can lead to disruption of the rest of the family's ability to parent the children. Routine checkups are the first line of health care that suffers, followed by attention to chronic health problems. This lack of attention, in turn, can cause such lifelong health conditions as hearing loss, speech problems, and even brain damage.

The Homeless Health Care Project in California (Roberts and Henry, 1986) documented the impact on children's health of living in unsuitable places. They found increased upper-respiratory infections among homeless children. Such ailments as bronchitis and pneumonia resulted from the living conditions homeless children experience, and what children are suffering in California is just what they suffer in Missouri, Massachusetts, and every other state in this nation.

Most of the health problems diagnosed in homeless adults can also be found in their children. Unable to bathe and wear clean clothes as they could if in their own homes, children are subject to skin problems. Without their immunizations, they can be vulnerable to childhood diseases which are avoided by children whose families take them for regular health care. The lack of such immunizations, in turn, can keep homeless children out of schools which require such health care as a prerequisite for attendance.

Education: Robbed of a Future

Homeless children are deprived of much that we, safe and secure in our own homes, consider commonplace. Education is a critical loss to homeless children. Without an adequate education, homeless children are not participating in the normal events of childhood and are missing their preparation for adulthood. If these homeless children grow up lacking an education, they will be ill-prepared to care for themselves as adults and their children.

All over the country, we are hearing about homeless children who are missing out on an education. States are now receiving some funding to investigate the problem of educating homeless children and are describing the special problems facing these children, even when their parents wish to have them in school. The United States Department of Education reported (February 17, 1989) to Congress that, according to the best estimates of the states, more than 65,000 of an estimated 220,000 school-age homeless children do not attend school regularly.

First of all, when children and their families are in the "mobility addiction" mode and are traveling around the country seeking answers to their problems, the children miss out on school in several ways. They don't stay in any one place long enough to get enrolled in school. After missing weeks at a time, the children are far behind their classmates even when they may be enrolled at last. Maza and Hall (1988) found that 43 percent of the school-age homeless children they studied were not in school!

Fighting for an Education

Of all the heroic efforts to receive an education the children in the shelter witnessed, probably the most memorable reported was that of a twenty-eight-year-old black mother, Joanne, and her fourteen-year-old daughter, Tanya. The two were easy to remember because they looked more like sisters than parent and child.

They became homeless when Joanne lost her job, and they were placed in a rundown hotel converted into a family shelter in Philadelphia.

Joanne, like so many homeless single parents, had minimal job skills and training. She had grown up in a family which consisted of her mother and three brothers. The family had lived on welfare. Her mother, an uneducated woman from the rural South, supplemented her welfare by cleaning homes and being paid in cash so her welfare check would not be affected. Even with that, the household income was inadequate to feed and clothe a growing family. Joanne frequently had to stay home from school to baby-sit her younger brothers while her mother worked.

The only social outlet Joanne's family had was the local church. Both Joanne and one of her brothers were gifted musically and either played or sang with the church choir. As the neighborhood they lived in changed for the worse, so did Joanne's brothers. One brother was shot and killed in a drug incident with two other young men. Her brother introduced her to the escape provided by alcohol and crack cocaine.

At age fifteen, Joanne was pregnant with Tanya. Having a daughter gave Joanne a reason to put her life in order. She wanted Tanya to have the opportunities which she had missed, especially an education. Joanne and Tanya lived in a small, furnished apartment in the city. Joanne found work in a convenience store at the edge of the city. She felt she was doing the best she could to raise her daughter and to provide for the two of them.

When the convenience store changed ownership, Joanne was laid off. The new owners could not afford any help outside the family. When she applied for unemployment compensation Joanne found, to her chagrin, that the previous owners had not paid any taxes and were wanted by the authorities. Joanne's money was running out quickly, so she had to seek help finding a different place to live.

Tanya had always liked school and was an average student. Joanne was determined to keep her in a familiar environment and decided not to transfer Tanya to a school near the shelter, a common practice among parents who try to keep their homelessness a secret. However, Tanya's school was at least an hour's walk from the shelter. Often, the pair would arise and dress by 6:00 a.m., eat breakfast at the shelter by 7:00, and start walking to school by 7:30.

Tanya was able to remain in her old school for several months until classmates and the school personnel discovered she was living in a shelter. Suddenly Tanya's status at school changed. She had to endure taunts by her classmates, some of whom had been her friends (so she thought). After one particularly painful put-down by a classmate who had once been a friend, Tanya struck back. She kept striking back at others during and after school. The school principal, sympathetic to Tanya's situation, nevertheless asked Joanne to transfer Tanya to a school near the shelter rather than suspend her for fighting.

With a heavy heart, Joanne enrolled Tanya in school near the shelter. Life had drastically changed for both Joanne and Tanya. Now, nothing they had found comforting and familiar was the same. Joanne's efforts to find work were unfruitful, and days would pass when she would merely sit around, almost silent, lost in her own thoughts. Recently, Tanya had noticed the smell of alcohol on her mother. Not surprisingly, Tanya soon stopped attending school almost altogether.

The impact of being homeless itself creates a poor self-image in homeless children, who are often ashamed of being homeless. All over the country, states are reporting problems associated with trying to educate homeless children. For example, in Tennessee the state has tried to design programs for homeless children, recognizing that these children need "someone to monitor them and show personal interest." The state found 789 homeless children with 372 living with friends or relatives and the rest in shelters, foster care, or other places.[1]

Sheila's Education

By all accounts, Sheila is pretty. She is a slender, light-skinned, Afro-American child. Most adults like this child because she is bright, articulate, and well mannered. Sheila was only eleven years old when she and her family arrived in Chicago's shelter system.

Sheila's family, her father, mother, and sister, lived with her grandmother for several years in an apartment. The family was on a marginal income. Sheila's father worked on construction when assignments were available. Sometimes he walked down to a corner about two miles from the apartment where moving companies would hire men for day work, loading huge vans with crates or furniture. Sheila's mother occasionally baby-sat other children, but mostly, she looked after her mother who was elderly and in ill health. Although the family had few worldly goods, they enjoyed being with one another. Even with her grandmother so sick, she always welcomed Sheila with a smile and asked about her day at school.

When her grandmother died, Sheila, her little brother, and both parents were evicted from the apartment complex. All the family owned was put out on the sidewalk where, in a matter of less than two hours, it was stolen or destroyed by others who preyed on the less fortunate. Sheila told a child and family social worker about the family's experience living on the streets of the city for five days, sleeping in subway-station entrances, parks, and on the street. She talked about seeing winos, prostitutes, and mentally ill persons—all in the same places where the family was trying to sleep for the night. Sometimes during the day, the family would go to the library where it was warm. Each morning, Sheila reported, they would get up, go to the nearest warm place to clean up, and then she and her brother would go to school!

Eventually the family went to the city-run shelters. For one month, they were housed by the city in overnight motels. This meant that they slept in the motel at night, but each morning they had to pack up their belongings and leave. All day long, the family had no real place to go, yet had to lug their meager possessions with them. Even at that, Sheila continued, it was better than sleeping in the park. "But," she said, "It was pretty scary there at night. Not everyone was nice to each other." Later the family was assigned to a permanent motel shelter run by the city where they have lived for over a year.

Somehow through all of this, Sheila's parents have kept her in school. As hard as it is to believe, Sheila has also maintained her place on the school honor roll! Despite the grief of losing her grandmother and the trauma of living and sleeping on the streets, Sheila insists that she was never scared because she knew that her mom and dad were always there!

Sheila will make it because her parents had the

strength and determination to stay together and to continue to reassure their daughter of their love.

The problems of these children present a special challenge to the schools. Homeless kids are far behind their classmates and need special attention, as well as other kinds of educational help, to succeed. Many schools report that homeless children need preschool enrichment in order to prepare to benefit from school. The children may require tutoring or other kinds of remedial help in order to catch up with their classmates. The homeless trauma means that many children need extensive counseling to make the transition from their deprived home life to a successful learning experience. In addition, they and their families need other kinds of support services from school social workers, counselors, and others.

The stigma of being homeless has a significant impact on children. They often feel shame and ostracism from the other children. School counselors and social workers are trying to help these children in a variety of ways, including keeping supplies of soap, shampoo, clean underwear, and the like, for the children to use. Writer Rene Sanchez wrote in the *Washington Post* (Dec. 19, 1988) about homeless children enduring insults, taunts, and ridicule at the hands of other children at school. School personnel talk about children being "heckled, even struck with rocks, while walking home."

The Stigma of Being Homeless

There is a tendency to blame homeless people for their condition. Homeless children are also blamed for situations that are out of their control. When the District of Columbia's city government decided to place homeless families in a large motel complex turned into a family shelter, it underestimated the numbers of homeless families who would require emergency shelter. Therefore, the facility was opened without regard for the special needs of the children who would be living there for long periods of time. It also underestimated the sheer numbers of children who, with their parents, would require shelter there.

The children talk about how awful they feel when classmates and their teachers tell them how bad they smell. This is because their mothers did not have money to buy detergent to wash clothes for the week. And, in some shelters, there may only be one or two washers for the entire shelter population. Frequently, these may be donated appliances which have already seen many years of service and are ill-equipped to withstand the pressures placed on them by so many families. If the mothers wash their clothes by hand, the problem of how to hang them to dry becomes an additional dilemma. Will the clothes be safe from theft? How can they dry without clotheslines? And what about bathing?

The children are also behind in school, usually because they move so often that they are seldom in a stable environment. But in school, they learn from the other children that they are "lazy" or "dumb."

The motel owner, under pressure from community agencies and other organizations, bought playground equipment for the 600 children living in the shelter. The equipment purchased was the kind most of us as average families might buy for our backyards. Certainly this kind of equipment was never meant to be used by 600 children daily. When the equipment was destroyed in less than one month, this situation was referred to as an example of how homeless children are destructive (Sanchez).

Other reasons homeless children don't come to school

are many. The noise and confusion which exists in many shelters is disconcerting for parents and children alike. Drug dealing, lack of a family routine, gangs in the shelters—all this creates an atmosphere of commotion and confusion. Parents and children literally can't get themselves together enough in this confusion to send the children to school, and a bewildered and frightened child, even one with good motivation and a delight in school, cannot properly clean himself and organize to reach the classroom.

The schools need to provide outreach programs to homeless parents, helping them to become involved in and supportive of their child's progress in school. With most homeless children moving frequently, it would be helpful if school programs had some continuity, so a change in school would not necessarily mean these children would have to adapt to entirely different learning programs.

Why don't homeless parents send their children to school? These parents may not value education or fail to send the children to school, in part, due to lack of proper clothing or immunizations or transportation. Many times the parents are so involved with the day-to-day survival of the family that education is, at the moment, not a high priority. When a family is in crisis, most of the adults' energy is taken up dealing with what is necessary for the family to live. There is little strength to deal with anything else, including school for the children.

When the parent, herself, is school-age, the problem of how to further an education while homeless is compounded. Without child care, the teen parent is unable to attend school. Even if care is provided, the homeless teen parent may lack the motivation or the self-esteem to the extent she does not consider attending school among her choices.

For this teen parent, her life script is already written. Without an education, she is destined for a life of poverty on public welfare, which is inadequate to live on in most cities of this nation. Coping with her problems uses up most of her time and energy. What is left for her baby? What kind of life will this child have? How can we, as concerned persons, positively help this young woman to rewrite her life script and that of her baby?

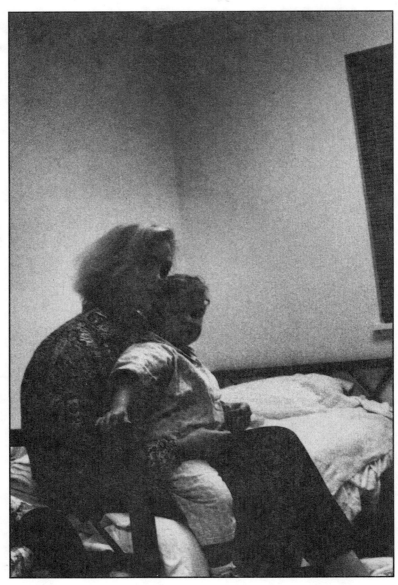

Shooting Back, Inc.

3

How It Happened: The Causes

When Children Are Homeless with Adults

Hall

The causes of homelessness are varied and complex. There is frequently more than one reason for the homelessness of an individual family. One of the primary causes is unemployment or underemployment of the adult or adults responsible for the child.

Unemployment

Unemployment looms large in the homeless scene. In the study conducted by Hall and Maza (1988) 21 percent of the homeless families included stated that they had been employed as recently as within the past month. Another 25 percent had been employed within the past three months. These families had existed from "hand to mouth" with little savings, or none, set aside for the proverbial "rainy day."

The families interviewed had almost identical stories. The paycheck would almost stretch to the next payday, but there was virtually nothing left over. In fact, for most of the families, the paycheck did not stretch far enough to cover all the expenses. These families would be called underemployed, with their income not adequate to meet their expenses. When unexpected expenses such as car or medical problems arose, the family simply could not pay those bills, plus meeting their other monthly obligations for food and shelter. For many families these troubles have been compounded by the parents' inability to plan any kind of budget.

When unusual expenses came up, the family's fragile hold on stable housing was often the first necessity to collapse.

Today, even moderate-income families are not immune to the specter of homelessness. For the two-parent family, where the father worked outside the home while the mother cared for the children, marital problems could be disastrous. We have heard countless stories about situations where a breakup in the couple led to the homelessness for the mother and children.

Washington Post reporter Claudia Levy described the situation of a mother and her thirteen-year-old son who were reduced to living in their car when her husband left her. The car was eventually impounded by the police, and the mother and son were forced to live in a shelter to keep from freezing in the winter cold. The reporter went on to describe the problems faced by moderate-income families when rental costs were on the rise faster than family income.[1]

And once a family is out on the streets, the ability to move back into a home of its own becomes more complicated. Most rentals require a security deposit and first and last month's rent. When you don't have enough money to pay the rent at your home and have been evicted, the problem of getting *two* month's rent, *plus* a security deposit, is absolutely out of the question. So the family slides into the morass of homelessness with little hope of being able to have a dependable home.

Diane: A Single Parent

All Diane ever wanted was to be a wife and a mother. Her own mother and father had divorced when Diane was three. Since then, she had seen her father only on a handful of occasions. Her mother had worked as a clerk in a department store for awhile and then had married her stepfather. Although Diane did not like her stepfather, she acknowledged that he at least kept her, her mother, and her two sisters together. Her mother was not a happy woman, Diane admitted, but, after one failed marriage, she was not going to give up this man. So, Diane and her sisters grew up in a household without much warmth or encouragement. Diane determined she was not going to end up like her mother. She would find "Mr. Wonderful" and have a happy home.

When she met Alex, Diane thought she had found Mr. Wonderful. She could not wait for her dreams. As soon as she graduated from high school, Diane and Alex married. At first, her dreams seemed to be coming true. Diane was a full-time mother with two small daughters and a husband who worked to provide for them. Even when Alex had an affair with a young neighbor, Diane forgave him and continued with her marriage. She wasn't going to end up like her mother, and, besides, what could she do to support herself and two children?

Being a single parent is not what Diane expected to be. The thirty-one-year-old, brown-eyed brunette had been living in Arizona with her husband and two children, Alaina, age six, and Stephanie, age nine. Her description of coming home one day and finding her husband molesting her daughter, then only eight, was gripping. She was frantic to escape from him and to protect her child.

Diane moved out of the house and into an apartment while she pressed charges against her husband. His arrest and imprisonment had a dramatic impact on the family's finances. Because she had married right out of high school, Diane had never worked at any kind of job except for fast-food restaurants. She found work at a dry cleaning firm which paid barely enough to cover rent and food. Her pay covered only the barest essentials. The counseling Stephanie needed after her trauma—although reduced in price because of the family income—nevertheless did cost per session and meant transportation expenses across town to the family-service agency.

The "last straw" was broken when Diane was laid off at her job. She thought about how she could "start a new life" and decided to move to Las Vegas where she had friends who could help her. She loaded the girls into the Chevette, sold some of her belongings, and with $350 set out. Like so many homeless people before her, Diane moved to a city where she had friends. Upon her arrival, these friends helped Diane find an apartment and to start seeking assistance from the social-service system. She was given emergency food and a voucher that could be used at a local grocery store while she waited for food stamps. She was also referred to a local agency which assisted her in the search for a new job or possible job training.

After sorting out her options concerning caring for herself and her children over the long term, Diane was able to enter subsidized housing, apply for AFDC for the children, and to become enrolled in a local junior college for business-administration training. She was finally beginning to plan for her new life. She was carefully watching Stephanie for signs that she might need to continue the counseling begun in Arizona.

Following through on all these sources of assistance has required a determination and stamina that not many of us could muster. Yet, Diane is still maintaining, "I know what I want for myself and the kids." And she is determined to make it.

Think about your own situation. How long could you and your family survive without a payday? Even with your paycheck, how do you cope with unexpected large expenses—the transmission conks out on your old car; your daughter is injured in an automobile accident and will require at least a month's hospitalization; your aging father who lives with you has become so ill that he requires skilled nursing care. These are severe problems for all of us, but they are multiplied for the homeless. It is impossible to provide for the basics with the loss of a single or at the most two paychecks. And with an inadequate paycheck, even the smallest emergency may be critical to the family's ability to keep their home.

Even when the family breaks up and the adult (usually the mother) is employed, she is frequently underemployed, that is, she does not earn enough money to cover the basics. A person earning the minimum wage for forty hours a week can hardly support himself, much less others! Most of us are aware that the basics are one thing and other unexpected or additional costs, quite another. For example, problems with the car can mean that some parents cannot get to work. Not making it to work, of course, can lead to being fired, which is a disaster for the struggling parent. Also, when that parent is not able to make reasonable choices about how to use what money is available, the problem is compounded!

Choices

Inability to Manage Money

As one talks with homeless families, it becomes apparent that some of their problems have come about or been worsened by poor choices of the parents. All of our lives are the result of choices we have made, as well as circumstances beyond our control. However, when a family is in a marginal position, because of being underemployed or because the paycheck is not adequate to meet basic needs and little else, the choices made by the person(s) in control of the money becomes critical.

When those choices are being made by a young person who has had little experience in managing or budgeting money, the result can be ill-advised. Impulsive spending by anyone, whether young or not so young, can make the critical difference between having a roof over the family's head or being on the streets. If you add the choices that include alcohol or other drugs, the problems for families increase dramatically. Children are then not only being threatened with homelessness, but they are also being parented by adults who are not in control of their own lives or decisions.

For most middle-class persons, occasionally spending money frivolously can sometimes be comical. Most of us have had times when we were lured into spending money on an item we really didn't need by a smooth-talking salesperson. Or maybe we were in a shopping mall and unable to resist that mohair sweater—on sale, no less. For most of us, such a silly use of our money would not mean the difference between paying the rent or being evicted. But that same impulsive behavior by an adult with children, who is barely squeaking by between paychecks, can make all the difference.

This kind of impulsive behavior is often seen by social workers who work with youth, teen parents, and families seeking help from other social agencies. Using their money for nonessentials is what adds to the negative reputation assigned to poor families who make unwise choices. Somehow many poor families always seem to have cigarettes and beer—sometimes liquor and/or narcotics.

Using Money Destructively: Drugs and Alcohol

Travelers Aid social workers relate many case studies about homeless families who lost their homes because of choosing to spend what money they had on drugs and/or alcohol. The tragedy of drug and alcohol (which is also a drug) abuse creates a sort of double jeopardy for the children of these families. First of all, they have a parent or parents who are unable to care for them properly. The desire for these substances clouds the parents' ability to care for the children, or sometimes even to remember that the children are there and have needs for nurturing. This story has become even more frightening when you consider the crack-addicted parent whose first and only desire is for the drug. Crack-addicted adults respond to a more-persistent call than that of their children, leaving their children neglected, if not also abused.

[handwritten margin note: horrible affects on children.]

Already we have documented the enormous lifelong sentence that parents bestow on their children when the mother uses drugs during her pregnancy. From alcohol to crack, the consequences may differ in the symptoms exhibited by the baby, but all are made even more tragic by the knowledge that they *could have been prevented!*

When children remain with their parents and accompany them into the streets, the neglect is intensified.

Away from familiar surroundings, the children are more frightened than ever.

Drugs in Shelters

One of the growing problems in some shelters has become drug addiction. The crisis of drugs in the shelter mirrors the problems of drugs on the streets of our communities.

At one family shelter in a large city, a fourteen-year-old girl approached one of the shelter workers because, she said, she wanted help. The girl told the worker about her drug problem—pills and cocaine. She wanted help but she was afraid the group of teenagers with whom she hung out in the shelter would find out she was going for treatment. She asked the worker to escort her outside the area so no one would see them talking. When she saw her friends approaching, she cut off the conversation.

The worker asked for assistance from the city Mental Health Association in trying to place this youngster into a drug-treatment program. The only program available had an eight-day waiting list. Although this girl clearly wanted treatment, eight days was a long time to expect an impulsive teenager, with a history of running away, to stay drug-free and on the shelter premises.

On the eighth day, the worker was to accompany the girl and her mother to the treatment program's office. The girl ran away on the seventh day and could not be found. She missed her chance to enter the program and to free herself from a life-threatening addiction. We don't know, but she may have missed her chance to reshape her future.

Family Violence—the Road to Homelessness

We have already referred to Diane and her road to homelessness following her husband's abuse of their

daughter. Other mothers and children are homeless because the mother is fleeing a husband who abuses
her—and usually the children as well—with beatings,
cursing, death threats, and sometimes torture. Women
who remain in such abusive situations generally have
poor self-concepts, sometimes believing that they
somehow "deserve" the maltreatment they are
experiencing—or either they stay because of sheer
fright. They have often grown up in homes where their
fathers abused their mothers, too. The family history of
violence and abuse is one that is regularly "inherited"
by the children growing up there and is often carried
into their homes to be repeated again. It is one of the
most "vicious cycles" imaginable.

When a mother summons up the courage to flee the
abuse, she is already at a disadvantage. Because her
self-concept is low, she is less able to locate a job (if she
doesn't already have one) than her more self-confident
sisters. If she has not been prepared educationally, or
with other types of job training, she may be able to find
only a minimum-wage position, not enough to provide
for the family as a single parent.

And where do a mother and her children go? If she
has a family—mother, father, aunt, uncle, grandparents,
other guardians—perhaps they can house her for a
while. But, if she must escape from a brutal husband
who is looking for her, it may not be safe for her and the
children to live with other family members or friends.
There are an increasing number of "safe homes," established by churches or social-service organizations
which provide a haven for victims of spouse abuse.
However, not enough of them exist to meet the need, and
they sometimes do not have enough funds to provide the
full range of assistance that these homeless families
need (that is, job training, educational assistance, child

care, and help for the children during this upsetting transition).

The woman who has the courage to leave an abusive situation for herself or her children may face homelessness as a consequence of her critical decision. Her children suffer in several ways. First, the role model of violence in the home is a "road map" for them to follow when they establish their own homes. Second, the need to hide for a period of time from the abuser can be frightening for all involved, especially the children. Third, the potentially resulting homelessness is, in itself, a scary and upsetting experience for children, even when they are not running away from violence in their home.

Family violence is a prescription for homelessness and emotional reactions in all the family members, particularly the kids. School can be disrupted with terrible results for the future of the children.

Inability to Get or Keep Steady Employment

The Kelly family is a prime example of what can happen to families when the parents cannot hang onto jobs. John Kelly worked in a factory in the Northwest. Although he was always praised by his employers for his attitude and ability, he still lost his job, because he lacked seniority, when the plant suffered a severe setback.

Pam Kelly is a pleasant homemaker who looks after the couple's four children and has prided herself on being able to oversee the family budget and maintain a household. The four children are two boys and two girls: Dave, a handsome sixteen-year-old, who is realizing his attraction to girls; Marty, an eleven-year-old boy who likes to tease his sisters, Sandy, age six, and Terry, age four.

After exhausting his unemployment benefits, John decided to try to search for work in another state. Pam was scared for him to leave and start out on his own. Pam had known other women whose husbands had left "so that they (the wives) could get aid." She feared that, once John was far away, the family might never reunite. So, the whole family loaded into the aging station wagon and set out.

For four weeks the family had lived in the car, camping along the road, while John looked for work in several Western cities. By the time they arrived at the family shelter operated by the Travelers Aid Society of Salt Lake City, the family was worn out, had less than fifteen dollars left, and was losing hope.

When I met the Kellys, they were living in a shelter which consisted of trailers grouped together near the overpass of two major highways. The playground for the children was a room-size, graveled area with a swing set. The trailers had one room, a bath, and a door! The families ate together in a common dining area in the one cinder-block building which also housed the bathroom, school, and any community services available. At that time, the shelter had a volunteer who would come in once a week and teach sewing to the resident families.

The Kellys had always lived from paycheck to paycheck. John never made enough money for them to save a penny, so when layoffs occurred, the family became desperate in a hurry.

With the help of a caring community, the shelter was able to provide such help as laundry facilities, a job search, and an on-site school for the children. John was able to find some "day labor" which helped the family begin to provide for itself again.

The happy ending to this story was: the Kelly family

was featured in a news story about homelessness, and John was offered a job with some long-term possibilities. The family was able to stay together and to become reestablished in another city.

Every year some five million manufacturing workers are permanently laid off as America changes to a service economy. That means many people who have always worked, and who want to work, find themselves without a means of livelihood. When benefits are depleted and yet no work is found, the slide into homelessness begins.

Criminal Behavior

When one of the parents in a family is found guilty of criminal behavior and sentenced to serve time, the rest of the family will likely be submerged in deplorable situations which have been described. Mothers with children may not be able to provide for the family, even with welfare benefits. Other kinds of problems already spelled out can crop up in this predicament. When criminal behavior is perpetrated by a single parent, the children are left with no one, unless a relative provides them with a home. As in matters of family violence, criminal acts usually alienate individuals from their families, so when the children (and perhaps the non-criminal parent) are left behind, there may not be a family-support system to step in and help them.

Mobility Addiction or Welfare on Wheels

We have seen instances where individuals cope with problems by continually moving from place to place. Those of us who have worked with teens in foster care have learned that, when they are faced with new situations or the results of their own impulsive behavior, they commonly react by running away. In fact, social workers can almost predict that during the first week of foster-care placement, the odds are that the troubled teen will react by disappearing. The rule for the worker has been, "Don't make personal plans for Friday night. You'll be getting a call about your latest client!"

With the increasing numbers of homeless families on the streets, that same coping mentality can develop. Families who are living in their cars, traveling from place to place seeking the answers to their homelessness, can fall into that same escapism. *If our extended family in this town can't help us, we'll move on to a friend's over in another town. And from there we'll keep on moving, looking for the answer to our problem,* they often think. Children in these mobility addicted families are rarely in any one place long enough to attend school and, therefore, fall farther and farther behind.

The stresses of living in automobiles, bus stations, or other places not suited for homes, leads to increased family turmoil and dysfunction. Parents under such stresses can become abusive or neglectful of their children—but, even when neglect or abuse are noticed and reported by social workers or other concerned individuals, help still may not be forthcoming.

It is extremely hard for public departments of social services to locate and plan for neglectful or abusive families who are on the road, only staying in one place for a day or two before moving on. These departments, already stretched to their limits by the urgency to investigate reports of child abuse and neglect by residents of the area, have few resources to track down mobile families in their jurisdictions. By the time the family is reported, it may have already moved on, facing new problems by doing so. They teach their children by example that the way to handle problems is to run.

AFDC, General Assistance, and Other Forms of Government Help: Do These Help?

What about our welfare system? Isn't it supposed to help keep families financially able to care for their children?

In the Hall and Maza study, Aid to Families with Dependent Children (AFDC) postponed homelessness for single mothers. Of the adults with children studied, 19 percent of the single women (contrasted with 41 percent of married women) became unemployed and homeless at about the same time. Seventy percent of the single women were unemployed first and then later became homeless with their children. It would appear the single parent who applies for AFDC is able to maintain a home after losing employment for a longer period of time than can the married couple where only one is the breadwinner and loses his or her job. But, since the family receiving AFDC benefits did in fact become homeless, it would seem that these public benefits are *not enough* to keep the family from becoming homeless. In that same study, it was likely when the man lost his job, which was usually better paying, the family became homeless more rapidly.

What about public housing for low-income families? Why isn't it aiding these families? Nationally, the supply of low-income housing is in critical shortage. For example, in New York City, there is a vacancy rate for low-cost housing of only 1 percent (Molnar, and others, 1988) while the wait for public housing is up to eighteen years! Only in selected American cities can a homeless family actually enter public housing without moving to the top of the list of waiting families, which is so long that the real possibility of ever getting in a public-housing unit is remote.

When the Parent Is Mentally Ill or Mentally Retarded

Children are not able to choose their parents, of course. When those parents are mentally ill or retarded, the children indeed suffer. Being born to parents whose ability to make wise and reasoned choices gives the child a better chance to grow up in a loving and stable environment. When the parents' ability to make choices is impaired, the child is at risk that the result of those choices will be a life on the streets.

Why Do Young People Leave Home?

Resener

According to Fred Grimm, author of *No Time for Fairy Tales*, there are short-term runaway young people and also long-term ones. Each are distinctive in motive and intention.

> Some teenagers are spontaneous runaways. They tend to respond impulsively to an immediate problem—a sudden conflict or blowup with parents, for instance. Many times the young person is back home within twenty-four hours.
>
> Parents often contribute unwittingly to this kind of behavior by venting anger and frustration through emotional threats. A parent can quickly cut off communications with a child and most of us, regardless of age or experience, react defensively and negatively to threats.[2]

There are situations in the home, however, that can

create problems to cause a kid to flee from home for a long time and even for the duration. Grimm notes:

> Many of the factors leading up to the decision to run away from home for an extended time may be found in the young person's home and school environment. Any one or more of the following problems may be a reason for a young person to be a long-term runaway:
>
> —He may have been subjected to prolonged periods of conflict with his parents and family.
>
> —He may be suffering from physical, sexual, or psychological abuse. Home has become unbearable.
>
> —He may have serious school problems such as consistent academic failure, intimidation by his peers or the inability to make friends. He just can't make it at school or with others of his age group.
>
> —He may have low self-esteem and is, therefore, easily influenced by peer pressure. He just can't stand himself, so he goes along with the street crowd.
>
> —He may have strong feelings of independence, with little or no communication with parents. He wants to make it on his own and feels no responsibility to discuss his plans with his parents.
>
> —He may be in debt or in trouble with the law. If he cannot pay off or is ashamed to face his family or the police, he may feel he has no choice but to keep running.

Why Do Young People Leave Home?

There are as many reasons to leave home as there are individuals living in the streets. Most of the young people I have counseled within our Anchor Home at the Nashville Union Mission (which provides a program of helping young men to get off the streets and back into the community) indicate that they ran away, even walked away, from circumstances they could no longer personally tolerate. There are several reasons, however, that seem to represent the overall reasons for leaving home:

Tension.—Quite a number are driven from their homes because of the tension that has built up between the members of the household. A young man told me that there was always fighting between his parents, who happened to be married divorcees. There was always competition between his father's children, of which he was one, and her children. Other young men have stated that their homes were always on the edge of "explosion" whenever finances, alcohol, gambling, and other issues were either discussed or experienced.

Terror.—A large number of young people, male and female, indicated that their reason for leaving home was due to abuse, physically, sexually, and verbally. Young women who reside at the Family Life Center, which is also a ministry of the Nashville Union Mission, have repeatedly shared stories of violent sexual and physical abuse from their parents and relatives. The news media continually reveal stories of sexual abuse by parents and relatives that keeps young people in a state of shock, guilt, and fear until they run in terror to avoid continued abuse.

Taunted.—There are young people living in the streets because they are more received as a member of the "street family" than they were within their own families. A young man commented, "Everybody made fun of me." Others indicated that they were always on the "short end of the measuring stick." "I was a loser to my own family," kids often confess. A young person told a counselor at the Anchor Home, "I ran away from home to prove I can make something out of my life." There are many young people on the streets who have a physical or mental deformity that was a cause of ridicule and contempt within the home he or she left behind.

Trapped.—Many young people depart because they feel "trapped" in an environment that does not allow individual expression. Often, a youth will run away because the demands of the parents make him feel like a prisoner in his own home. "My parents wanted to dominate me religiously and demanded a certain line of education. They determined what I was going to become, regardless of how I felt about it," another youth emphasized. I have talked to many young people who revealed in retrospect that they should not have walked away from their homes because they now realize that their parents were right in wanting to set up guidelines for their lives. This groups is most easily convinced to return home.

Taken.—Sometimes after a divorce case is settled, a parent who lost custody of the child in the family will kidnap the child and flee to parts unknown. The modern-day example is Dr. Elizabeth Morgan, Washington, D.C., who hid her child with friends from her estranged husband for fear that the husband would sexually molest the child. She was even jailed for refusing to divulge where she hid her child. For almost two years, this child did not have the love of her parents and lived a secluded life, which might have terrible consequences on her in the future.

Also, due to particular religious convictions, some parents, when their child is facing serious medical problems, have fled with the child into seclusion to avoid allowing their child to undergo necessary blood transfusions, operations, or other medical procedures. These children are not only cheated of sensible medical help to overcome their illnesses but are also denied the comforts of the home and friends during the time they need support and consolation.

Thrill-seekers.—Many a kid has left home looking for "thrills." They believe that their home life is dull, meaningless, and old-fashioned. Like the prodigal son in Luke 15, they leave home for the "fleshpots of the world." "I wanted to have a good time," a young drug addict told me, explaining why he left. I have heard those exact words hundreds of times. Like the prodigal son, they too end up in some type of "pig pen," if not the graveyard.

Travel.—Some young people leave home just to travel the world. Due to the cost of travel, most cannot travel beyond the sum total of their piggy-bank savings and end up stranded in the streets. Their intention is not to hurt a soul. They simply want to see what's on the other side of the mountain. However, many who see what is on the other side of a good home wish desperately they had stayed put.

Teasers.—Some leave home in order to tease or manipulate their parents into giving in to their demands. I have heard many youth admit that they left home "many times" to "teach Mom and Dad a lesson" or to "soften their attitude or restrictions toward me." The teasers say, "My parents love me, so if I threaten to run away or actually do it, they will give me anything I want to keep me home." Whenever I hear this, I have wondered why the parents did not leave home! At least the results would not be as disastrous.

Tricked.—Some young people are "tricked" by others to leave home. Led to believe that there is a "Camelot" life ready to be enjoyed away from home surroundings, many young people are willing to follow the advice of others who just want someone to run away with. Easily influenced by others, some young people find them-selves in difficult places, victims of their own inability to think for themselves.

Throwaways.—The saddest reason for young people leaving home comes from those who woefully say, "Dad didn't want me. He threw me out of his life." In homes where there are financial problems, lack of living space, and conflicts within the family structure, the parents plainly indicate there are "too many living under the same roof." "I felt like I was not wanted," many a young person put it, "so I left home," and the saddest part about it is that "Dad (or Mom) didn't come looking for me."

Running away was supposed to be a solution. They had no idea of the indescribable horrors they were about to experience.

4

Existing—Not Living—on the Streets: The Consequences

Part 1: Homeless Children and Their Parents

Hall

Living in the streets has serious consequences for adults, but it is worse on children. We are literally "losing" an entire generation of children not only because of what they experience by being homeless but by what they miss out on by being homeless.

Ellen Bassuk, Alison Lauriat, and Leonore Rubin wrote about their interviews with 116 homeless mothers, eleven homeless fathers, and 205 children living in homeless shelters and welfare motels in Massachusetts.[1] In the shelters they visited, over 90 percent of the families were headed by women on AFDC. The researchers described the pattern of family instability these mothers and their children had encountered before ending up in their latest shelter. In the year before coming to those shelters, the mothers and their children had moved an average of four times. You can imagine that many of these mothers had grown up in dysfunctional families where they virtually had no stability. They had always known disrupted, unstable lives—and now they were able only to provide their children with more disruption and more instability.

Shooting Back, Inc.

Anger and Homelessness: Its Impact on Children

Distraught and angry, Marge called the Travelers Aid office from a local hotel. Her car had been stolen over the weekend. It contained all of her important documents including her driver's license, her four-year-old son's birth certificate, and other vital papers.

When the worker and her supervisor arrived at the hotel, Marge was still awfully upset. Like so many, she felt no one wanted to help her—all social service agencies were useless. She had been moved four times in the past two months and had been asked to leave several shelters because she had broken the house rules.

While the social workers counseled with Marge, four-year-old Kevin clung to the supervisor. Marge, by this time, was screaming and yelling about how awful and uncaring agencies and shelters were. Meanwhile, Kevin, talking with the supervisor in the corner, said "Mommy's a little mad." He had precious few toys, and the ones he had were not appropriate for a boy his age. He occupied himself by playing a game of filling a glass with water, pouring salt into the glass, and trying to drink it.

The social worker suggested that Marge come into the office so they could sort out her problems and make a plan to help her. Later, the worker found that Marge was known to several agencies in the city, but she needed assistance in coordinating her sources of help. She even refused to consider help for Kevin. Instead of working with the TA social worker to develop a plan for finding permanent housing, Marge stormed out of the office, pulling Kevin behind her, ranting about how no one wanted to help.

Marge never came back to Travelers Aid, but the following week a report of physical abuse was filed against her at the hotel after Kevin was heard screaming by a neighbor.

Bassuk and her colleagues described the impact of homelessness on the children in the Massachusetts shelters and welfare motels. They talked about, "a three-month-old baby (who) was depressed, listless, and unresponsive; a fourteen-month-old baby (who) was unable to crawl or to vocalize even simple sounds."

The children I dealt with in the Travelers Aid offices and shelters were scared, depressed, angry, hostile, and even suicidal. With nothing permanent in their lives, they were growing up with no sense of a place to call home. They were learning that they were not very important in the scheme of things, that maybe they were even worthless. Naturally, their concept of themselves was poor. Even though some of their mothers were trying their best to provide for them, these children often did not have even the slightest basics for sound growth and development, regular and nutritious meals, routine medical care and immunizations—not even a regular bedtime in their own bed!

What kind of adults would these children become? Would they cope with life by "moving on" when hardships arose? Would there be a beloved Sunday School teacher who would help them to realize that they have a loving Father who would provide stability in an unstable world? Would these children in the streets become the adults in the streets of tomorrow?

Kid in the Middle

Generations of women were living in the Connecticut household: Louise, the great-grandmother works in a cafeteria and is a pleasant, mature woman; Louise's thirty-seven-year old daughter, Jane, who is a born-

again Christian after twenty years of free-basing cocaine; Jane's nineteen-year-old daughter, Tina; Tina's
five-year-old daughter, Kristine, who attends kindergar-
ten.

Jane had recently begun to feel that her family, as well
as the world in general, was against her. In spite of her
family's reassurances, her sense of rejection grew. Feeling unwanted in her mother's home, Jane snatched up
Kristine and fled to New York where she applied for family shelter and AFDC (Aid to Families with Dependent
Children). When Jane could not produce documentation
to prove she really had legal custody of Kristine, the
public welfare worker and the shelter providers referred
her to Travelers Aid, asking that we help sort out the situation and help her to find the documentation required.

It was a while before the TA worker could gain Jane's
trust. Jane finally gave the worker the phone number of
her home in Connecticut. You can imagine the relief
that Tina and Louise felt when they learned that Kristine and Jane were safe, and they wanted both of them
back home again.

Jane was almost relieved about sending Kristine back
to her mother and great-grandmother, but she herself
was not ready to return. She was "tired and needed to
think of herself." After arranging to transport Kristine
home that very day, the TA social worker consulted with
the shelter case manager and the public welfare supervisor about Jane's financial and emotional needs. Financial aid and a psychiatric evaluation were arranged
to help Jane deal with her paranoia and plan her return
home as soon as possible.

For a child who is living in a world where nothing is
steady or stable, even the day-to-day routine of living in
a shelter becomes a substitute for the comfort of a per-

manent home. When that home, however, temporary or chaotic, also threatens to change, it can be almost more than a child can bear.

David and the Move out of the Shelter

Because of the growing numbers of large families needing emergency shelter, at one point District of Columbia officials decided to move all families consisting of only one parent with one child in Capitol City Inn (shelter) out of the shelter. Throughout the day, a city government van would drive up to the shelter and load the mothers, children, and their plastic bags with their clothing and a few toys, and drive away.

Most of the families did not know of their impending move until a couple of hours before they had to catch the van. Many of the mothers had no means of contacting friends or family about the move or where they could be reached before they had to climb into the vans and go. Most of the mothers were young (about eighteen to twenty-two years old) with small children. The shelter where many were being relocated was for overnight occupancy only, which meant that early each morning, they would have to pack up all their belongings and carry both the belongings and their child around all day until they could return to the shelter at night.

That move from the Capitol City Inn had a horrid impact on the children as well as their mothers. Homeless children, who may have already moved several times before they and their mothers have entered the shelters, are missing their social-support systems—grandparents, friends, and neighborhoods. They are fearful of change and are closely tuned in to the anxiety of their mothers.

One worker described watching one little boy, about

six or seven years old, sitting on the backseat of the van while his mother loaded the large green plastic bags full of their possessions. The worker could tell that this child had no idea of where he was going or what was about to happen to him and his mother. Fear glinted in his dark eyes.

From behind the van came three fellows about the same age as the boy in the van. One of them looked up and blurted out, "Hey, look, David's leaving. David, are you going away?" At that moment, huge tears fell from David's eyes and trickled down his face. As the van pulled off, his little friends just stood in the driveway, and David never looked up from his lap.

Part 2: Homeless Adolescents

Resener

A young person having lived in the streets for some time is unlikely to bring gifts from the souvenir shops. A father of a young teenager, who had run away from home and had lived in the streets of a far-off city for nearly a year, told me that his daughter had come back. I could sense that, even though his daughter was home again, the father had mixed emotions about it. I said to him, "You don't seem very happy over your daughter's return. What's wrong?"

He replied, "I'm happy she's home, but, boy, is she a mess!"

I asked what he meant.

He replied, "We have her off the street now, but it is going to take some time to get the effects of the street out of her."

The effects of street life do not end when a young person—who has been living there for any length of time—voluntarily or involuntarily goes home. The hurt and hardship of street life run hard and deep in a person's mind and body.

W. A. Criswell, in his book *With a Bible in My Hand,* tells of a man in the days of Queen Victoria who was sentenced to life in prison for a crime he did not commit. A friend on the outside, convinced of his innocence, worked untiringly for the man's release. Finally, after years of research, the friend found the information he needed. The man made his appeal before Queen Victoria herself, and won his case. Queen Victoria signed the pardon for the man in prison. With gladness and joy, he went to the prison, entered the cell where his friend was incarcerated and cried, "Look, I have your pardon. You are a free man . . . your pardon has been signed by the Queen herself!" Instead of a joyous response, the prisoner lifted his shirt to exhibit an ugly, devastating cancer. Gazing into the eyes of his liberator, the prisoner snorted, "Go ask the Queen if she can heal this."[2]

Getting the young person off the street is one concern; getting the young person rehabilitated from the streets is another concern of great importance. The young person, whether he comes home voluntarily or involuntarily, brings with him problems created by the life-style of the streets. There must be "debriefing time" allowed for the young person who has returned home in the same manner as a soldier is given time to "debrief" himself of wartime activity. From what I have heard from the stories of those returning from the streets and those soldiers returning from the war zones, their stories parallel a great deal as far as the threat to life is concerned.

Physically

Homeless young people suffer significantly from the lack of proper nourishment and consistent eating habits while living in the streets. Many young people return home with hollow eyes, loss of weight, scars, diseases of all kinds, malnutrition, undernourishment—all the evidences of a hard and harsh life-style.

A young man from the Anchor Home in Nashville, Tennessee, writes, "I had to depend on others for food and shelter. My appearance got worse. I didn't care about the length of my hair or what clothes I wore. I lost respect for myself." It is thought that self-respect is the first quality a street person loses. As a street person once asked me, "Why should I worry about how I dress? I ain't going nowhere." This attitude shows up at the home of a returning young person as well. It is a severe problem to overcome.

Mentally

Soap and water may remove much of the external evidences of street life, but they will not remove the mental complications created by street life. These are the wounds that must be dealt with by "tender loving care." Psychologically, a young person who has been in the streets quite a while can really become "messed up."

Disfigured Minds

It only takes a short time on the street for a young person to realize that he is surrounded with unpleasant sights and unexpected proposals. *The mind* is bombarded with the cries of despair, desperation, and defeat. *The eyes* see beatings, rapes, crime, defeated lives, perverted graffiti. *The ear* is exposed to filthy expressions of activity, sensual laughter, and jokes, cruel and disgusting proposals; one's total life is surrounded by a perverted life-style where decency, kindness, and goodness are soon stripped away. Even a short time on the street can swallow up a person's total being in an atmosphere of perversion. It is nigh unto impossible to erase the mental aberrations created by living in the streets. The comforts of home cannot easily eliminate what the young person has seen, heard, and experienced. Still, the comforts of home may be the best solution to the troubled mind of a runaway.

Distorted Minds

A young man reported that, upon returning home, the first words from his father were, "You are not to do the things here at home that you were doing on the streets." Most returning runaways meet the same type of warnings when they cross the thresholds of their homes. Survival on the streets can foment distorted life-styles—a mixture of acceptable and unacceptable activities. Most young street people practice "situational ethics"—"what works for me is acceptable." These young people become involved with life-style patterns that are acceptable only on the streets. For survival purposes, many young street people resort to crime, prostitution, drugs, lying, stealing, and other antisocial behavior.

However, when returning home, all of these activities are supposed to cease. It is not easy to change habits, even when survival is not an issue. I have heard of parents telling the returning runaway, "Don't talk about your time on the streets to your brothers and sisters. We don't want them to try it for themselves." Parents of returning runaways must be aware of the distorted behavior their runaway has based his survival upon and be willing to help him adopt new behaviors on which to build a new life.

Distracted Minds

Bill Cosby, in one of his television ads calling for the

support of black colleges, stated, "A mind is a terrible thing to waste." Literally, this is what a street runaway is doing. A young person who removes himself from the normal flow of society and chooses to live aimlessly on the streets actually causes his mind to cease growing toward maturity. It is certainly possible for a runaway person to be twenty years old with a fifteen-year-old mind because of the lack of proper education and development of the brain. Many returning runaways have found out that education, which develops the brain, stopped when they left home and that their level of thinking and acting is below that of their kid sister who stayed home and continued her education. It is, of course, disconcerting and disappointing to the parents of a returned runaway with the mind level which he had when he left months or years ago. They do not have a diploma for "street education" when a runaway chooses to go home.

The street runaway's mind has been occupied just in surviving, perhaps diluted by drugs and alcohol, subject to obscene images and perverted ideas, a target of fists, stones, and iron pipes, as well as a void of enrichment through education and positive experiences. No wonder the father, previously mentioned, commented concerning his daughter, "She's really a mess!"

Disfigured Minds

The sum total of the mental ability of the runaway when taken off the street is likely to be totally dysfunctional. In other words, the returning runaway is a misfit in about every phase of home life. The time away from home has virtually made him a mental misfit, to the point where he finds himself mentally out of place in the home where he was raised. His thoughts, ways, affections, and aspirations are so far out of line with the rest of the family that he is likely to run back to the streets that treated him like a family member.

Spiritual Problems

Of course, a runaway on the street any length of time finds himself or herself facing moral temptations. Many runaways violate their morals or have them violated within a few days of living out there.

"It's use or be used," a young lady remarked as I confronted her life-style. The result is that runaway children carry within them the emotional consequences of having been disgraced and defiled willingly or unwillingly.

These emotional traits can be handled while living on the streets because "everybody is doing these things," and there is no one to judge or criticize another's behavior. As long as one's behavior does not interfere with another's behavior, there are little or no challenges such as: "You're going too far" or "Maybe we shouldn't do this."

One is generally in control of one's conscience while living on the streets. He either ignores his conscience or has the ability to hide his inner feelings when engaged in immoral behavior for the sake of survival. However, when he contemplates leaving the streets or actually leaves them for home, he is confronted with what he has become while there.

Many of the books available on runaways, in my opinion, go too far in exploiting the life of the runaway. In some instances, I believe these books are literally "spiritualized *Playboy* magazine material." In one book I read, the author, who was a runaway, actually wrote out her sexual experiences that read like pornography. Too many previous books written on runaways center on sexual misbehavior to the extent a runaway is automatically listed as "whore, slut, pervert, sexual whoremonger"; thus, the reputation of the runaway precedes him or her back home, and this is where the guilt, shame and anger are part of the "mess."

Most young runaways return home with shame due to the life-style they experienced on the streets. As he left the mission to go home, a young person told me, "It's going to be rough facing Mom after all the things I've done." He said, "Brother Resener, I wasn't brought up to live like I've been living."

Young runaways returning home figure that everybody by now is aware they ran away from home. Whether at school, church, or work, people have perhaps labeled them as some type of "sexual playground," and those kids simply cannot handle it. Many do not cope with the "silent accusations," nonverbal innuendos, so, rather than face the shame, they run away again.

Guilt

Many runaways carry a heavy load of guilt, whether they remain on the streets or return home. One of the impacts of guilt is low self-esteem. This is beneficial if it produces humility and contrition and sends the guilty person to God for forgiveness and restoration. However, if the person does not experience relief from guilt, he will have a low estimate of self and will reveal it through patterns of inferiority and perhaps severe antisocial behavior.

Some runaways back home are so down on themselves that they see no chance of ever being happy or healthy again. They begin to question their activity on the street by asking, "Was it all that bad that I really had to do what I did to survive?" Even if the returning runaway finds the parents willing to forgive, it is still tough for many of the runaways to forgive themselves and get on with life at home.

Anger

"Why don't they understand that I had to do what I did?" pleaded a young man who was going home after being in our Anchor Home program. Yes, he was going home, but he felt as if his parents resented being associated with a runaway. Many young people go home angry because they sense that everyone will accuse them of being selfish, irresponsible, and inconsiderate. Many who return home are angry because that is somewhat of a defeat in their attempt to live away from home, regardless of the reasons for running away. Even when a runaway returns voluntarily, there can be anger in that. "It didn't work out" the way he thought it would. This is more prevalent in the runaway who is brought home in a police car. He believes everybody will treat him inconsiderately rather than accepting his reasons why home was intolerable as in the cases where physical and/or sexual abuse existed. A runaway may also return home with anger over the fact that his home was not like other homes where the "kids down the street" liked their home and didn't want to run away.

Shame, guilt, and anger are deep-seated emotional problems that can only be answered through forgiveness. There are three areas of forgiveness the runaway must discover for a total recovery:

• Forgiveness from *God*—available through the Lord Jesus Christ.

• Forgiveness of *others*—available when we forgive "others" for what they did to us.

• Forgiveness of *self*—available when we are able to forgive ourselves for behavior unbecoming as an individual.

Not only is the runaway to seek forgiveness in this manner, but all the other family members who are directly involved in the life of the runaway.

Deficient in Job Experience

The runaway may also find it hard to land a job once he goes home. Street life does not make a resumé appealing. As in all job applications, "Where have you worked in recent months?" is essential. Few employers are willing to hire a young person who has spent the last few months or years living on the streets. The returned runaway may face rejection in the labor market or accept a low-paying position which offers nothing more than minimum wage. Many have high hopes of a good-paying job; however, the wasted time living on the streets make it practically impossible for them to be hired so they can be on their own. Parents of returning runaways must be willing to help with their education as well as their living expenses. It is not unusual for parents to have a child who stayed away from home for several years that is just finishing high school with their financial assistance.

Criminal Record

It is almost impossible to live on the streets without having trouble with the law. There are few honest occupations a young runaway person can engage in, so one begins stealing, selling drugs, and even selling oneself in the sex market, all of which is illegal and thus leads to a jail sentence. A large number of runaways have criminal records, and, even though as juveniles their records are locked up and they can even be discharged upon good behavior or at the age of adulthood, still the runaway must carry the stigma of being a convicted criminal.

As he returns home, the guilt and shame of being a convicted criminal, of having spent time in jail or another type of correction facility, begin to fill his head and heart and give him an inferiority complex. Even though the record of incarceration may be secret or expunged, the runaway bears the shame and experience of having been locked up. According to many runaways, jail is the worst place to be when parents are looking for them.

Loss of Role Models

Perhaps the worst consequence of living on the streets away from the influence of the home is the inability to establish a home for oneself. Life on the streets has no "home structures" that one can carry into adulthood. Having left home, for whatever reason, a young person cannot live out the prominent roles of the home because he or she has not been under the influence of the major role models of the home, that is, father and mother. It is hard for a young person to assume authority in his own home when he did not grow up under authority. Having no father or mother role model to look to, the young runaway will find it difficult to manifest the role of a parent when a child is born into the family. He or she may want to be a good, effective parent but usually comes up short of being a quality parent, and the results are seen in their offspring.

A prominent movie star was once visiting a coal mine

in Kentucky. Dressed in a lovely white dress she made her way into a mine shaft. As she proceeded into the tunnel, the superintendent of the coal mine suggested to her, "Ma'am, I wouldn't go down into the shaft with your lovely white dress."

Startled, she replied, "What is wrong with me going into the shaft? What's wrong with my white dress?"

The superintendent answered, "Ma'am, nothing is wrong with you going into the shaft with a white dress. It's only that it won't be 'lily white' when you come up out of the shaft."

The tragedy of street life is that scarcely anyone comes off the streets without some of the street's dirt, degradation, and defilement. Preventing a young person from becoming a runaway is far better than being able to clean up the physical, mental, spiritual, and social "mess" attached to him after living on the streets.

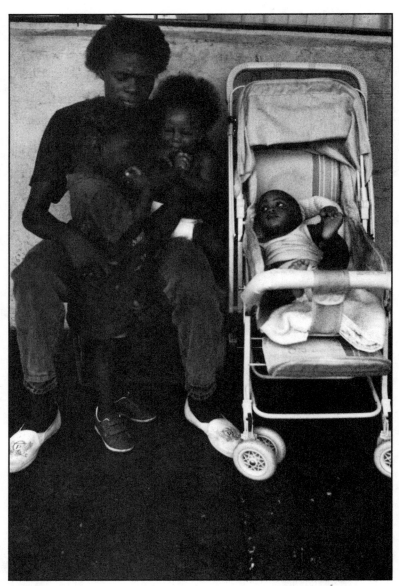

Shooting Back, Inc.

5

Distress on the Street—The Conditions

Homeless Children and Their Families

Resener

"I just couldn't take it anymore," cried a mother with two children who sought refuge at our mission's Family Life Center. "For years I put up with my husband's abuse to me and the children, so I gathered up as much money as I could, wrapped up my children with the only coats we had, bought tickets with the money I had, going as far as the money would take us." Her money brought her from a Midwestern state to Nashville, no doubt a safer place for her children and herself, but I am afraid that's all the money accomplished for her.

Her story is typical of the many abused women who come for refuge or are escorted to the Family Life Center. Also typical is the fact that most abused women leave an intolerable situation without plans or preparation, thus placing themselves and their children in a vulnerable position.

Strange as it may seem, in many situations the consequences of running away may—and actually—have resulted in a worse situation than what the mother and her children faced at home.

"America's refugee camps are the shelters and motels

in the large cities that house the homeless poor. Children growing up in these surroundings are exposed to some of the most criminal and vile elements of our society. They confront apathy, deprivation, abuse, and violence daily. *What can we expect from children growing up in such a situation?*"[1]

Thus, Jim Hubbard asks a heartbreaking question in his observations about homeless children, "What can we expect from children growing up in such a situation?" My answer is simply: You can expect nothing more than the situation they live in will allow. What is the perspective from a child's point of view as he or she lives in homelessness?

To find out what it is like living on the streets as a homeless child, I followed the mother and her two children throughout a day of activity. I tried to envision what the children saw and heard as they wandered among the homeless population in our city. As they left their small and crowded apartment room we had provided for them at our downtown center, they saw men sifting through the garbage cans; they witnessed a drug sale; they heard a "drunkard's song" from an intoxicated group of street winos.

As they passed down the streets, they heard the cat calls directed at their attractive mother; they listened in on a conversation of a local "pimp" who drove up to the curb and asked their mother if she would be willing to do a "trick" for "some hamburger money for the kids." Walking past an alley, they saw a group of men kneeling around a crap game; they heard the filthy language of the gambler's plea for a successful roll of the dice; further down the alley they were exposed to the nakedness of a mentally deranged person.

As the day wore on, they were greeted by a group of

fellow homeless persons who invited them to join them down at the river where they had built a little village of huts and bivouacs. One man in the group offered to be the "protector" of the family of three. As they reached the center of town they were honked at by angry drivers who felt they should walk across the intersection at a faster pace. The rushing crowd bumped them to the outside of the sidewalks; most of the people walking by them on the sidewalk glanced the "other way," trying to pretend that the family was not there or that the mannequins in the store windows were more appealing than the shabby, wrinkled appearance of the family of three. Jostled, ignored by the downtown crowd, the family headed back toward the mission where the pace is slower, where a homeless family of three blends in with the rest of the homeless population.

In following the family of three, I came to the following conclusions:

1. They were not *safe*, even though they fled from their home for reasons of safety. They walked in potential physical danger, and vulnerable to riff raff who prey upon those, such as the mother, who live in despair and desperation. In the past I have counseled fearful, frustrated women who have been asked by every pimp and drug dealer in town to participate in their perverted lifestyle for "the sake of your children." Their agony is traumatic, especially among those who gave in to those immoral hucksters.

2. There was no *stimulation* beyond the desire for their safety. A homeless person told me that walking the streets is like walking an eternal "dead-end" alley—few flowers, fewer yet kind words of communication. Disgusting graffiti, obscene figures and suggestions, beer and liquor ads fill the empty spaces of building walls;

expressions that deepen despair rather than console and comfort a distressed heart. As one homeless person put it, "There isn't enough alcohol in the world to help me forget my troubles." "How can anyone be inspired to be anything living in the streets?" a woman asked me when I confronted her about her shady life-style. "It's bad for me to have to live on the streets; it's worse for my children," a lady angrily reminded me. "See any leaders here you want your child to follow?"

My able assistant, Rev. Richard Kritsch, once re-marked about the existence of the homeless child, "After a while it will become a way of life with them." He is so right it hurts, and that is why we must come up with solutions for families with children, while they still desire to overcome their obstacles and leave the streets. Otherwise, the family in the street will lose all hope of finding an appropriate place in a community.

Hall

Capitol City Inn

Capitol City Inn is a motel in the northeast section of Washington, D.C. It is well known in the city because it is now the largest shelter in the District of Columbia for families and children. The shelter is located in a business district at an intersection through which thousands of people drive daily commuting to their downtown offices. The District government acquired the use of the motel through an open-market process, which means that the government pays an exorbitant amount of rent, reportedly over two million dollars per year, to the motel owner for use of the premises.

On any given day at Capitol City Inn, the shelter population consists of 190 to 200 families. Children in the shelter number between 500-600 daily. The children range in age from newborns to eighteen years old, with the majority of the children being around elementary-school age.

The most striking reality of shelter life is the lack of space. There is a lack of space for children to play, study, or to have a quiet time. Every inch of space available in the shelter is used for living or for the social service providers. Many of the families consist of parents and between two to six or more children all living in one small motel room. The grounds and the hallways of the shelter are covered with dirt, sour milk, trash, and bits of food.

It can become a family crisis for these children to attend the schools around the shelter. All of the area schools are at least a mile or more away, forcing the children to dodge rush-hour traffic to cross streets. Certain paths along their routes are perilous because of taunts and threats from other children due to their homeless status. Rather than continue to fight and overcome, well over 50 percent of the homeless children in this shelter retreat and make it their only world—a world without education.

Physical Problems

Physically, children on the streets suffer as do their parents. Report after report indicates that living on the streets is harmful to children physically and emotionally. Let's start with the physical effects of living in places other than one's own home.

First of all, without proper "climate control," children become more susceptible to all the usual upper-respiratory ailments—colds, bronchitis, infections, ear-aches, and so forth. Many of the children in shelters or other street arrangements have "colds." That is, they have constant runny noses, coughs, or other such symptoms.

In a normal home setting, we would put these children to bed with plenty to drink and some sort of medication. Without that "normal home setting," the homeless child may not even have a bed to rest in, especially during the day. If the family is living in a shelter where everyone must leave during the day to return in the late afternoon or evening, there merely is no place for the child to rest. While the family is living in a car or other space, there may be no resting place, or only one which is crowded with the rest of the family—a recipe for spreading the ailment to everyone else in the family.

Newborns or small infants are particularly vulnerable under these kinds of living arrangements. Being homeless is literally life-threatening to these little ones.

The *Washington Post* on Independence Day, July 4, 1989, reported the second death of a homeless child in three days. The first child was an eighteen-month-old who died as a result of a fire which broke out in one of the city's large motel shelters for families. The second child was a four-month-old baby girl who was found unconscious by her mother early in the morning in a temporary shelter for homeless families.

Physical hygiene deteriorates when the family lives under makeshift conditions or in shelters. The lack of a place to wash up or bathe may mean that children and their parents are not able to keep clean and are, therefore, more vulnerable to bacteria and viruses. Without a "place to call home," illnesses ranging from minor to more debilitating may go untreated. This means that minor problems become major before anything is done about them.

Families may wait to seek treatment for ailments until the situation requires an emergency response. Adults dealing with the day-to-day survival of the family may not be able to focus on what seems to be a less-serious physical ailment until it becomes so serious that it cannot be ignored.

Nutrition

Several researchers have talked about the problems of a proper diet for homeless children (Bassuk, et al; Rowe, 1986). Some shelters, especially motels turned into family shelters, lack any place to prepare food. Further, many do not have feeding programs which means that families must leave the shelter to find prepared food, often fast food.

Even if they have cooking facilities, the shelters may not have a place for homeless families to store food. This can be a particular problem for families with infants who are on formula or milk. Federal subsidies to families to buy prepared food or food to cook for themselves have been limited to under one dollar per person per meal. Try to feed your family on this amount every day! It's terribly difficult even when one knows a lot about nutrition and has the means to cook their own meals at hand!

Emotional Health

Living with your family as a homeless child is hazardous to your emotional health. Travelers Aid social workers report that nearly always the children of the homeless family mirror the level of anxiety and frustration experienced by their important adults. The kids may be overly aggressive, demanding, or unable to focus their attention on anything for very long. On the other hand, they may be withdrawn, uncommunicative, and overly dependent upon others.

"It's scary here at night, and I miss my dog," confided one little girl in a family shelter. Constant anxiety and fear are common elements of life in the streets, even when you have important adults or parents with you.

For years, those of us who worked with refugee children noticed that they were smaller than others their own age who had not gone through the same sort of traumas. They were also behind these other children both physically and emotionally. The same situation is true of homeless children. They have developmentally regressed behind their peers. They have the proverbial two strikes against them. They display a wide range of stress-related symptoms as well as physical illnesses (Bassuk, et al.).

Social workers who have worked with children in foster care have seen many of the same problems I have described with homeless children. It's as if we have a continuum of problems which beset children when they are deprived of a stable, nurturing environment. It goes something like this:

1. *Optimum* condition for proper growth and development. This condition is found in a stable home where the child is loved and protected by parents or other adults. The child is helped to grow and develop in an atmosphere which affirms the child's self-concept and encourages the child to become all that he or she can be. Many foster-home situations try hard to provide this.

2. *Less optimal* but provides shelter, food, and education. This condition is exemplified by foster care. Even with loving and nurturing foster parents, the child is still deprived of his or her parent who, no matter how abusive or neglectful, still occupies a significant role

with the child. The child's nutrition and health may improve, but he or she may still show signs of developmental delay in school or in physical growth. Emotionally, the child may be coping with the aftermath of abuse and neglect or the hope that everything at home can be corrected and he can return.

3. *Even less optimal* condition. This is discovered with most of the children who are homeless but with adults. Their physical and emotional needs become secondary to the family's need for survival. The children display emotional, social, and physical lapses as well as physical problems from living in this condition. Of course, educational development delays are not uncommon.

4. *Least optimal* condition. This is the condition of homeless youth, those without parents or other significant adults. It is similar to the problems experienced by refugee children, particularly those who are unaccompanied minors. Survival conditions apply—these children often have to use desperate means to survive. When children become homeless after spending years in foster care, their resemblance to refugee homeless children is striking. They literally have no home to which to return.

Social Relationships

A child with a homeless family on the road has few opportunities to make friends with children their own age. In fact, there may be little or no chances to make friends with *any* other children. Even in the shelters, parents may be so protective of their children in such a setting that they do not permit them to socialize with other children there.

Even at school, a homeless child may feel like the proverbial "outsider." Ridiculed by their peers at school, homeless children may simply withdraw, not reaching out to anyone else either at school or in the shelter. When that homeless child is with adults on the streets, traveling from place to place, school may be little more than a day here and there on the winding road to somewhere else. Again, there is no time for friends.

After a childhood of being on the outside, never being part of the group, the homeless child can grow into adulthood without the social skills to make friends, particularly lasting friendships. And what about the kind of relationships that lead to stable and lasting marriages? Are we setting the stage for weak or failed relationships throughout life with the seeds being planted during a childhood of homelessness?

Just Plain Fun

The mobile homeless, especially those seen by the Travelers Aid agency workers, do not have room in their cars, vans, or other means of transportation for many toys for their children. Available toys may not be suitable for the children, in poor condition from being crammed into the car or under the seat, or nonexistent!

The social worker looked through his desk to find a couple of toys for the kindergarten-age boy and his newly walking toddler brother. While the worker talked with the parents, the boys were to play on the office floor.

After a few minutes, the worker noticed that the toddler seemed bewildered and almost in tears. "What's wrong?" asked the worker.

"Well," remarked the boys' mother, "We've been living in our car for the last six weeks. This is the first floor that our little guy has been on in a long time. He's forgotten what a floor is."

Shelters for families usually put a premium on available space. There is little or no room for recreation inside or outside. Usually, with so many people living in such close quarters, rules may dictate that children remain quiet in the common areas. But children need to play. If they do, being picked on or exploited by older children is a real problem for them. Self-esteem suffers under these conditions.

DC's Homeless Parents

The Mental Health Association of the District of Columbia became interested in the coping abilities of homeless families, especially the children living in a shelter environment. In order to assess the special needs of homeless children, a survey was taken of the parents of the 190 families living in one of the city's homeless shelter hotels.

The families were asked a series of questions on how they were helping the children to survive that environment. It should be noted that homeless children, particularly the ones in this kind of shelter, are overexposed to drugs, alcohol, violence, school dropouts, and teenage pregnancies.

Many of the parents responded that, in order to shield their children from the vices of living in the shelter, they did not allow their children to meet and mix with other shelter kids. These parents took or sent their kids to school each day and, when the children returned, made them spend the rest of that night inside the room. This cautious measure of isolating their children from everything around them was the only way these parents felt that they could protect them.

Not surprisingly, the children always longed for their old neighborhoods and friends. Many of the parents noted that the children experienced changes in eating and sleeping habits. Also, most of the parents reported that the children living in the shelter were more hostile and angry than they considered normal. All that would appease the children were assurances from the adults that their stay in the shelter was only temporary. So, many of the parents who had virtually no hope of locating another place to live felt they must lie to their children to keep their hope alive—even when their parents had none!

Perils Facing Street Kids

Resener

A young person living in the streets is unlikely to write home, "Having a good time. Wish you were here." Street life is the other side of the coin of misery for those who make city streets their home. If home life is intolerable, then street life is worse. Street life is the epitome of frustration, shock, and despair in which one sometimes can actually envy the death of a companion.

Street life offers an alternative to home life, but it never provides the answers to the problem young people left home to resolve. Those who ran away from violence at home found out all too soon that there was a more severe degree of violence in the streets. Those who fled home because of "demands" placed on them in order to be a part of the family found out there was a steep price to pay to "belong" in the street family. A girl confessed to me, "On the streets you use others or allow yourself to be used to survive."

The average street person will find himself in worse bondages and handicaps than he thought he was under while living at home. On the streets he must worry about hunger, shelter, clothing, diseases, and even death. He must decide how to meet these situations.

Street life does not offer many options for survival; actually there are only two—"use others or be willing to be used."

A young person named Ralph, who lived in the streets of New York City for several years, spoke about the conditions of street life (*Street World*, 1989).

> I was on and off the streets since I was fifteen or sixteen years old. My reason for being on the street so much was because I would either get into an argument with my mother and she would throw me out or I would just leave.
>
> While on the street, I did anything from hustling [selling his body] to selling drugs to taking things from stores to sell so I could either get a hotel room to stay the night or just so I could get some food in my system.
>
> Basically, what I am trying to get across to you kids is this: Before you think about leaving home to please yourself think it over twice to make sure you are doing the right thing for yourself. Life on the street gets you nowhere, but either dead or behind bars in a jail cell. Before you leave home please think about it 'cause you're probably gonna wind up regretting it later.

No matter how severe a situation at home may be, the potential runaway is not prepared for what he will face by running from home to the city streets.

The streets do not *provide* free meals, lodging, clothes, and the like. Most runaways do not consider the financial burden they may face by running away from home. Dad or Mom may have been abusive, violent, or irrational, but in most cases they did pay the bills. When one leaves home, one must pay one's own way. This is where realism shatters any prospect of making it on one's own on the streets without becoming involved in some bad trouble.

The streets of the city do anything but *protect* anyone

from harm, diseases, or even death. In fact, living in the streets exposes the runaway to as many, if not more, incidents of violence than were experienced at home. The runaway is vulnerable to anything evil and negative that street people experience. In San Francisco, "the casualties are many. Street kids die quickly and quietly. More than 5,000 teenagers a year are buried in unmarked graves."[2]

Youth Worker reported:

> The violence young people face every hour is staggering. Some are repeatedly raped. Girls are often kidnapped, drugged, raped for weeks at a time. Many kids on the street live under the power of a pimp who beats them if they come up short, talk back or try to run away. Fifty percent of the kids served by New Orleans Covenant House last year were physically or sexually abused; half of those were hospitalized.[3]

The streets of the city do not *present* a favorable lifestyle where a kid can better himself. If one does make it living in the streets, he has probably compromised to the extent that the only thing that hasn't changed is the color of his skin. The streets of the city actually prescribe only one type of life-style—"use others or get used."

The streets of the city, of course, do not *prevent* young people from getting into serious trouble because of the survival-of-the-fittest life-style they must develop. If drugs were not a problem at home, they will be once a young person is out there on the streets. If they were not introduced to sexual abuse in the home, they will be on the streets. If fighting and arguing were offensive to them at home, they will have to be accepted if one makes the streets his place of habitation. If stealing and lying were not accepted at home, the street kid will soon discover that much of his life is produced by lying and stealing since there is no way a young person on the streets can obtain and hold a legitimate job.

The streets do not *produce* character that enables a young person to live above the negative aspects of homelessness. The characteristics of street behavior strip away innocence, self-esteem, and individual pride. This is one of the main reasons why runaways do not relish the idea of returning home. Many runaways end up being sexually violated, manipulated by others, and, in some situations, for the sake of survival, become willing participants in the degenerative activities of street life. They feel in their hearts that they are less than what they were when they left home. Some even commit acts of abuse and violence they accused their relatives of back home. It is almost unthinkable for them even to consider returning home, so they continue their existence on the streets rather than face relatives and friends.

Let's hear from a young person called "Precious K." (*Youth Worker,* 1989):

> When you're out there, things are very hard. You're not sure which way to go. Some kids are runaways. Some are thrown out. But whatever the reason they're in the streets, they are out there and it is no joke. When you get off the streets things are better, you're more calm, things are more organized in your life. You can get a job because you are not tired and rundown. Things become more clear in your life, you achieve more hope to get things done. You feel better about yourself. The thoughts of suicide decrease and fade away.
>
> When your chance comes to get off the streets, please go. Even if it's back home to Mom and you know things

are gonna be rough, take it in stride and please abide by
what your parents say 'cause at the end it'll pay.[4]

It is a tragic commentary on our country's vast social
resources and services that in most cases the streets of
the city are the only available options for young persons
who have been in trouble at home.

6

Put the Blame Where?—Profiles

Part 1: Homeless Children with Adults

Hall

Lack of Affordable Housing

Elena is a thirty-one-year-old Hispanic woman with a nine-month-old son. She had been homeless in a large Florida city, but she came to a New England city seeking housing. The Travelers Aid social worker helped her enter a homeless family hotel while she applied for Section 8 housing. Elena had been frustrated with the lengthy process of applying and waiting for this housing. Even though homeless families are moved to the top of the list in this city, the wait can still be long as several years!

Because Elena is a bright woman, the other residents in the homeless hotel consult her about other services in the city. Elena has quickly become knowledgeable about what is available to homeless families and is willing to help her neighbors. She has even joined a local women's homeless advocacy group, trying to feel that she has a certain amount of control over her life.

From time to time, Elena becomes depressed, feeling that the housing system is working against her, resenting the lack of privacy or space in the single hotel room she shares with her son Manuel. In spite of her depres-

97

Shooting Back, Inc.

sion, however, she is still able to maintain an open and healthy relationship with Manuel, a thriving and energetic toddler.

Sometimes, Elena's frustration with the system and her depression work against her. She has been known to become enmeshed with illegal activities as a means of survival. Recently, she was caught selling stolen goods in the hotel, and she and Manuel were thrown out.

She cries when she talks about trying to settle down in her own permanent place and being a good mother to her son. The social services in the city can only do so much for Elena. Her social worker can try to help her feel better about herself and not be so depressed, but Elena is indeed living in a depressing situation with an interminable wait for conditions to improve.

Trying to fix the blame for the complex situation we call homelessness is akin to describing nuclear physics in a single paragraph. It simply cannot be done. The reasons for homelessness are multiple, from failures of the federal government to assist in the development and maintenance of affordable public housing to the counterproductive choices individuals have made to the traps of alcoholism, drug abuse, and other antisocial behavior.

Let's begin by talking about one of the most obvious problems: *the lack of affordable housing*. The reasons for this lack have been cited by experts from The National Alliance to End Homelessness:

• Increasing rents and growing numbers of households unable to afford nonsubsidized rents, and

• Increasing imbalances between the demand for and the supply of low-income housing.

All of us have observed that the cost of rent has risen

meteorically. In fact, today the cost of rent as a percentage of our income is at its highest rate in twenty years. The number of poor people, those with incomes below the poverty line, has risen dramatically. Today only 25 percent of those below the poverty line live in public housing or subsidized rental housing. All this is happening at a time when the need for low-income housing is far exceeding the supply.

Putting these facts into perspective, it means that those families living from paycheck to paycheck, when faced with any kind of financial emergency, can lose their homes. Finding another home they can afford may simply be impossible!

As far back at the 1949 Housing Act, the U.S. set a goal for affordable and decent housing for every family. Multiplied homeless individuals and families are evidence that we have not met that goal. In fact, we are seeing more and more families doubling (and tripling) up in order to have a roof over their heads. These "couch people," as they are being called, may represent a number ever greater than those already out on the streets.

In Fairfax County, Virginia, where I live, there are innumerable jobs. The unemployment rate is about 3 percent. Each week the papers are full of advertisements for jobs ranging from technical and professional opportunities to service jobs requiring little or no skills, or even the English language. Yet, in the parks of this, one of the most affluent counties in the nation, there are *employed* families living in tents while working here! They earn reasonable wages but cannot afford the cost of housing here. There is no affordable housing for the employed, let alone those families on welfare!

The problem is severely critical now, but within the

next few years, the situation is likely to worsen. By 1995 more than 300,000 units in developments built under programs backed by the Housing and Urban Development Department (HUD) in the 1970s could come out from under federal-rent ceilings. In addition, another 636,000 units rented under Section 8-program rent restrictions could return to the open market. About 12,000 of these units could return to the private market in the early 1990s, according to the National Advisory Council of HUD Management Agents.

In many cases, the prevailing rents are double or more those of the federally protected units. This means that when they are returned to the private market, many thousands of low-income families will be forced to move out of these units and literally onto the streets. When we already have thousands of homeless families who are unable to find affordable housing, the idea of even thousands *more* is dreadfully frightening!

In the state of Maryland alone it is estimated that 11,000 families could be forced from their apartments as this book is being released. Linda Parke Gallagher, executive director of the National Low Income Housing Preservation Center, said, "The federal government reneged on its part of the deal with private developers when it curtailed the low-income housing tax credit program in the 1986 tax law" (*Washington Post,* April 2, 1989).

Because developers can prepay their forty-year federal loans after twenty years, there are developers eagerly waiting to prepay their loans and go to the open market with their property. Some of the properties are in areas which are undergoing "gentrification" and there are yuppies standing in line to obtain some of the

Section 8 housing that, twenty years ago, they would have considered totally unacceptable. So, only in those areas of the country that have not undergone considerable real-estate appreciation are the federally underwritten properties reasonably secure for their low-income tenants.

No Housing

Rosalyn is a forty-two-year-old black woman with an eighteen-month-year-old daughter, Lanay. Rosalyn and Lanay were evicted from their apartment in November. Rosalyn was able to find a family shelter during the cold winter months.

By February, Rosalyn was able to obtain a certificate for assisted housing and found a suitable, affordable apartment. After the necessary inspection by the housing authority, all that remained was for the landlord to sign the papers. On the day of her move, Rosalyn learned that the landlord had refused to sign and did not offer any reason. Rosalyn was overwhelmed with anger, feeling that the landlord was discriminating against her because of her gender, her color, her welfare status, and her being a single mother.

This anger spilled over onto her housing search worker and others in Rosalyn's world. She needed an outlet for her anger so it would not immobilize her. She had become afraid to trust others for fear of being disappointed. She stopped looking for another apartment and seemed to care less for Lanay.

Rosalyn needs a genuine friend who will help her to focus her energies on parenting and finding housing. Like so many irate, frustrated homeless persons, Rosalyn is "stuck" in a world of mistrust and anger. Perhaps a friend and advocate could help.

Primary Causes of Youth Homelessness

Resener

Only two reasons emerge as we seek the primary causes for young people living outside the home: the parent(s) or the young person. The parent too often places blame on the young person. "He or she doesn't appreciate what we've (I've) provided for them," the parent complains emphatically.

The young person counters with, "My parents don't understand me."

The young person may confide, "My parent(s) abuse(s) me."

Parents often say, "We cannot control him."

Listening to both sides makes it complex to delineate the origins of youth living outside a home. One must conclude that in a given situation there are times when the parent(s) is (are) responsible for their kids living outside the home; at other times it is clear that the young person deliberately removed himself from the family setting.

The Bible abounds with stories of families with internal conflicts that led to a young person's leaving home. Maybe we can discover reasons for their departure that apply to our present-day phenomenon of displaced youth. We may accomplish two aims with a review of these stories: *prevent* an increase of displaced youth by identifying the problems that send youth away from home, and *correct* existing problems in both the parents and the displaced youths so the family can hopefully be reunited.

The earliest biblical story of a runaway youth deals with Jacob, son of Isaac (Gen. 25). The household of Isaac was marked by godliness, humility, and the birth of two sons, Esau and Jacob. Though Jacob was the second born, he was destined by God to receive the family inheritance over Esau, the firstborn. All Jacob had to do was wait for God to fulfil the family blessing, which would have made Jacob rightful heir to the position and possessions of the home. However, Jacob, whose name meant "deceiver" or "supplanter," could not and would not wait until his father's death. Twice he and his mother instigated deceitful schemes to obtain the family blessing.

The first scheme dealt with the hunger pains of his brother, Esau, who had come in from the field after an unsuccessful hunt. Besides being a deceiver, Jacob was a "kosher chef" and demanded from Esau his position as "firstborn" before he would serve him food to offset his hunger. Yielding to his stomach, Esau reluctantly gave Jacob the position of firstborn. This caused a severe rift in their relationship.

It was bad enough for Jacob to con Esau as he did, but in the second scheme to obtain the actual bestowal of the birthright his mother became involved to assist Jacob, probably for her own preservation, for it now appeared that Esau had shown that he was not qualified to head up the family or to be the keeper of the family inheritance. Genesis 27 reveals the story of how Jacob and his mother created a plan to misrepresent Jacob as Esau to Isaac the father. Isaac thought he had blessed Esau with the birthright, when actually it was Jacob who had disguised himself as Esau. When Esau discovered the irrevocable deception, he became murderously angry, and Jacob was warned and encouraged by his mother to run away from home quickly.

In that case a mother and a son contributed to the family separation. I often hear a young person say, "I was always in the middle of the family argument. I was either to blame for the problems, or I always had to take sides. I got tired of being the family football, so I left home." All too often parents will use a child as a bargaining chip or blame the child for the family's problems. Parents often place a child in deceptive schemes to achieve their own selfish purposes. In such cases young people sense that they must show favoritism toward one parent against the other. A runaway youth said, "When I couldn't love them both without a conflict, I decided not to love either of them and left!"

Jacob himself had to share part of the blame for his separation, due to his constant deception of Esau and his father Isaac, until it was impossible for him to remain at home. He left because of his own acts of deceitfulness. Some young people can't go home because of their rebellious and deceptive actions. In a repentant frame of mind, young persons have said over the phone, "Mom, I'm sorry I acted the way I did." Only when a young person admits that the fault is his for being on the streets, away from home, is there any hope for better things for that family. I am referring only to cases where it is partly or all the fault of the child.

As Dr. Hall and I have pointed out, in many cases children have been unjustly "sent packing," kicked out, expelled from their homes, often through no fault of their own.

The sad ending of the story is that Jacob had to leave home, never to see his parents again. The mother never saw her son become the head of the family. Some twenty years later Jacob and Esau were reunited, but not without fear and suspicion on Jacob's part. Jacob still lived in fear of being killed by Esau. I want to believe that Jacob could have had it all—family blessing, possessions, had he waited for God to work it out in an orderly manner. Instead, he lost it all, just like some kids on the street today. They can never go back home because of the conflict that still exists between the parents or the young person will not change behavior and life-style.

Another account involving a runaway person is that of King David and his son, Absalom (2 Sam. 13—19). David also had a daughter who was sexually assaulted by her half-brother Amnon. In revenge, her brother Absalom caused the death of Amnon. Fearing for his life, Absalom left home and lived for three years in another country. David, his father, would not seek Absalom or permit Absalom to return home. After much persuasion by friends, David allowed Absalom to return to his hometown, but with one restriction: he was not even to visit his father's palace. "[He can come back, but] I don't want to see him" (2 Sam. 14:24, GNB). Absalom came back and for two years did not look upon his father's face. After two years Absalom begged to be received by his father, who finally agreed to the reunion. After five years of separation, father and son were reunited. One would think all was well between Absalom and his father, but the worst was ahead of them.

Five years of separation and hardship had turned Absalom into an unforgiving person who led a rebellion against his father and nearly usurped the throne. In a final battle against Absalom and his army, the king's soldiers overpowered them. Thus, they not only put an end to the rebellion but to Absalom's life.

I have often wondered what would have happened if David had followed Absalom and tried to work out an agreeable ending to the killing of Amnon. Yet, David chose to let Absalom stay away from home for three years, and when he permitted Absalom to return, he would not see him for over two more years. Not much of a reception for a runaway! I have had fathers tell me over the phone, "I'm glad my boy is at your mission, but don't send him home. He's not welcome here."

Often, as in the life of Absalom, rejection breeds acts of crime. A sadder note to this series of tragic events is, when informed of Absalom's death, David the father unashamedly broke down and cried, "O, my son Absalom, my son, my son Absalom! would to God I had died for thee" (2 Sam. 18:33). David's expression of his love for Absalom was genuine, but too late. Like so many fathers, David waited too late to show his love toward a wayward child.

Many times at the mission I have been involved in such incidents toward the wayward. One of the most tragic incidents occurred when a runaway girl was brought to our shelter for women. She was several months pregnant. Living in the streets, undernourished, lacking proper health guidance and provisions, she was extremely ill and eventually died, taking her baby with her. Her parents came to Nashville to carry the body home for burial. I can remember the expression of grief on the father's face as I told him of her stay at the women's shelter. I can still hear him lament, "We should have come sooner while there was a chance."

The life of Joseph (Gen. 37—50) reflects the tragedy of internal problems of jealousy and resentment that often take place in the home. Joseph was one of twelve sons born into the household of Jacob. From his early childhood days it was obvious that Joseph was gifted in the matters of God. Unintentionally, Joseph provoked jealousy and resentment toward himself as these special gifts unfolded in his life. Joseph's family was in the business of shepherding. During the time when his brothers were away shearing sheep, Joseph's father sent him, with supplies, to them. As the brothers saw Joseph approaching, they plotted to rid themselves of him. First, they planned to kill him but then changed their minds. Finally they settled on the idea of selling him to Ishmaelite slave traders who were passing by en route to Egypt. With Joseph abducted to Egypt by the slave traders, the brothers returned home to tell their father a lie of how Joseph had met up with a lion or a bear and had been killed.

The story of Joseph's plight has at least two aspects. The first was the jealous brothers, who for the rest of their lives had to live with their consciences aflame with guilt, shame, and fear. They became an embarrassment to their father. They were considered troublemakers throughout the area. They adopted the traits and temperaments of their father, Jacob, and thus their own home life was tainted with strife. Only after the death of their father and the reassuring forgiveness of Joseph did they finally have peace within their hearts and homes.

Joseph's life itself took many twists and turns after he was sold to the slave traders and was carried to Egypt. Throughout the years of being a servant to Pharaoh, time in prison, and administrator of Egypt, Joseph never used the personal treatment he experienced by his brothers as justification to live immorally. In fact, quite the opposite was true. His cruel treatment did not make him become less than he ought to have been. Contrary to so many who had to leave home and allowed the street to corrupt them, Joseph remained moral and upright, even if it did cost him two years of his life in prison. He did not permit Potiphar's wife to lower his personal standards of character and conduct.

Joseph's life is a strong statement for overcoming the

temptations of being away from home. Young people today often yield to the seedy enticements of being away
from home. They yield for one reason or another, but
with a strong character and a positive outlook on life,
one can survive the perils of the streets. Joseph's life is a
glowing example that one can have character on the
streets and survive.

We must reach the young person who lives on the
streets with the message that one merely compounds
one's problems when he allows the philosophy and character of the street to assume control of his or her life.
Young street people must realize that becoming a drug
addict, a criminal, or a sex object does not "get even
with an abusive parent" or "get revenge on life" for what
has happened to them.

I am afraid that much of the hurt a young street person has experienced comes from the young person's attitude of "I don't care." The overwhelming truth about
Joseph's plight is that, though he could not control the
events that sent him away from his home, he could and
did manage the outcome. While his brothers were living
as losers, Joseph was living as a winner. That is the
message we must somehow convey to multiplied thousands of homeless youth.

Summarizing, one can make the following conclusions:

A. There are several types of parents who contribute to
   the reasons young people run away from home:
   1. Those who create situations that drive young peo-
      ple from their home—situations such as physical
      and sexual abuse, violence, drunkenness, over-
      bearing, and divorce.
   2. Those who are so legalistic concerning religion,

finances, courtship—"my way or the highway."

3. Those who are so meek and weak regarding leadership that, for the lack of authority, the young person walks out on the home without fear of discipline. Here you might remark, "The child left home in search of a father."

4. Those who are stoic in their reaction to a young person's leaving home. When discovering that the child left home, the parents close the door by saying, "He made his bed somewhere else. Let him sleep in it" or "He walked out on me. He knows where I am."

5. Those who, by virtue of the poverty and dysfunction of the family, literally "push out" their children as soon as they seem to be old enough to care for themselves on the streets.

6. Those parents who are so rejecting of their children that they "throw them away."

B. There are several types of young people who contribute to the reasons why they leave home:

1. The *selfish*—"I want everything my way. If you love me, you will give me what I want."

2. The *self-willed*—"I want to live my life as I want to. It's my life!"

3. The *sensual*—"I don't want authority. I want to do as I please."

4. The *searcher*—never satisfied. "Why can't I have a home like Bill or Sue has?"

Years ago an intriguing study was conducted concerning two families in Northampton, Massachusetts. One family head was a preacher, Jonathan Edwards. The other was a wastrel named Max Jukes. Jonathan

Edwards married a devout Christian girl, and from their union came 729 decendants. Of these, 300 were ministers, sixty-five were college professors, thirteen were university presidents, sixty were authors of books, three were United States congressmen, and one was vice-president of the United States. Most made a significant contribution to society.

Max Jukes, who lived near Edwards, was not religious. He married an unreligious woman and from their union came 1,026 descendants. Of these, 300 died early in life, 100 went to prison for an average of thirteen years apiece, 200 were prostitutes, and 100 were alcoholics. The descendants of this man cost the state more than a million dollars to care for them.[1]

The analysis of these two families demands the question, *What type of a foundation is it that determines the type of life an individual will live once that individual begins to make his own choices?*

A cartoon showed a mother kangaroo with a baby peeking out of the pouch. This caption was at the bottom: "His mother determines his point of view." It's true. Like no other factor in a child's life, the parents will determine his or her point of view in life. Like father, like son. Like mother, like daughter.[2]

What a child becomes is largely determined by the parents' behavior and attitude towards the essentials of life.

Lyle Schaller, in his book *Understanding Tomorrow*, identifies one of the characteristics of our age to be excessive expectations of institutions. "To a substantial degree, we parents have turned over to two institutions, the school and the church, the responsibility to develop our children into dedicated, dependable adults. Tests reveal that these expectations placed on our children far exceed their capabilities. Institutions were meant to supplement what we do in the home."[3]

The home is where love, honesty, dependability, faith, and compassion are taught.

James Dobson writes of a study on the early childhoods of inmates at a state prison in Arizona. The researchers were hoping to discover a common characteristic which the prisoners shared in hopes this would give some insight into the cause of antisocial behavior. Initially, the researchers assumed poverty would be the common thread. Such was not the case, for the prisoners came from many different socio-economic levels. The one fundamental characteristic shared by the men was the absence of adult contact in their early home lives. As children, they spent most of their time in the company of their peers, or alone. The conclusion of the study was that there is no substitute for loving, parental leadership in the early development of children.[4]

Josh Billings, the American humorist, once said, "Train up a child in the way he should go, and walk there yourself once in a while! Home is one place where actions speak louder than words."

A young lady wrote a letter to her pastor, Brian Harbour, telling him about the influence her father had on her within the home. She concluded the letter with, "I have a good solid concept of God as my Heavenly Father. And the reason I do is because of my earthly father. It's because of Daddy that I am able to love God and to relate to him as my Father."[4]

7

Help for Homeless Families

Hall

You Can Make a Difference

Excitement can certainly result when people, government, communities, and organizations care about homeless families and children. Together we can effect a change in the lives of homeless children, a change that is positive and in keeping with our values that each person is worthy of respect and dignity.

What Can the Federal Government Do?

The whole question of public housing and its funding is one that must be addressed by the federal government. The first step is to "fix up" the existing public housing—repair it and make it livable again where it isn't. When you drive through impoverished areas of major American cities, you can often see boarded-up housing that used to be available for families. After years of neglect, the units fall into incredible disrepair. They become unlivable, even for families whose need for shelter is so urgent that they will move into any place that resembles a roof over their heads. According to the National Alliance to End Homelessness, there are about 1.35 million units of public housing. Even this number

Shooting Back, Inc.

is far from enough to house the growing population of poor and homeless families. For those units which could be made rehabitable, the necessity for repairs is imperative, so homeless families can move in.

Then government at all levels needs to expand support for the development of additional public housing, more units of affordable housing for families and children. Even if the government decides today to support the development of massive numbers of public housing units, it would require years for these units to be built. We need not only to take this step but look for specific short-term solutions to prevent the loss of an entire generation of children who are forced to grow up in the streets.

There have been innumerable examples in which the federal government worked with local residents of public housing to make it possible for tenants to own their units at a cost they can afford. A number of national stories have focused on Kimi Gray, the welfare mother who lived in rundown public housing where crime and drug traffic had predominated. By organizing her friends and neighbors in the project, Kimi accomplished what seemed to be the impossible. She helped to organize the effort of ordinary, poor families to regain control of their homes. Through her efforts, today the project's residents have driven out the drug traffickers, reduced crime, and developed day-care, job-placement and many other services. Today most of the residents have jobs and pride in their neighborhood. Further, they have worked out a program with their government landlords to purchase their homes, and all this was accomplished by a partnership between the government and one determined individual!

In the U.S. today there are about 800,000 families

whose housing is subsidized by the federal government through Section 8 vouchers and certificates. Another two million live in housing that was constructed through federal assistance. A considerable amount of this kind of housing may begin to disappear within the next few years.

Housing that was developed with assistance from the Department of Housing and Urban Development (HUD) and Farmers Home Administration mortgage-subsidy programs are becoming eligible to be repaid over the next few years. If and when those loans are repaid, the owners can then use the property any way they wish, and many are unlikely to continue its use for low-income housing!

Housing that was constructed or rehabilitated under Section 8 program subsidy contracts is also scheduled to be retired over the next fifteen years. If the owners of these units do not continue with the program, we will lose about three quarters of a million low-income units, and, you guessed it, those poor people will be on the streets!

When Communities Care

Although I never thought I would come to this conclusion: our government needs to develop additional single-room occupancy (SRO) housing for single individuals or small families. In the past, the SRO represented the worst kind of housing imaginable to most of us. Run-down tenements housed the winos, the alcoholics, and all those people who "didn't fit" with the rest of us. Because the housing was run-down, cheap, and on "the other side of the tracks," few of us ever saw the residents who paid by the day or the week.

Then along came gentrification: fixing up the rundown, old houses and turning them into architectural miracles! These miracles, however, displaced all those people who lived on the fringes of our society and put them out onto the streets. Now, those of us who care about what happens to homeless people want those cheap units back. Some sort of home, even if it's a single room, surely beats the streets as an alternative!

The "No Time to Lose" program in New York state was not designed for homeless children alone but represents a state effort to provide a comprehensive, preventive program for black and Hispanic children. The program's long-range goal is "rebuilding the infrastructure of inner-city communities." It organized public, private, and voluntary sectors of the community to:

a. Strengthen families and communities
b. Promote economic self-sufficiency
c. Reverse school dropout and failure rates
d. Assure quality health care
e. Address the child-welfare crisis
f. Develop affordable housing and promote neighborhood renewal
g. Stop the cycle of family violence.

By banding together in a broad partnership, the city of New York is addressing the needs of these vulnerable children by working toward the prevention of homelessness where each of the problems identified above exists.

Real People Who Care

One person *can* make a difference in the lives of homeless children and their families. One such person is Tipper Gore, wife of Senator Albert Gore, Jr., (D-Tennessee) who is also a mother, an author, and an advocate. Her involvement with the homeless began in

1986 when her children asked her about the homeless persons they had seen on the street in the nation's capital. They were dismayed that adults could drive away and leave people on the streets with no place to go.

Deciding to put action behind her kind words, Tipper began to organize her friends to form an organization called Families for the Homeless, which raises money for the homeless. She is providing an example for her children of how one person can help make the world a better place for others, just as Tipper's mother had taught her.

We all can't be Tipper Gores, but we can all be role models of caring for our children and our neighbors. We can all become "our neighbor's keeper." Even on a seemingly miniscule scale we can make a difference in the lives of others.

Not in My Backyard

We have heard talk about the NIMBY syndrome—that is, the "not in my back yard" response when the community needs to locate facilities for the homeless in a neighborhood. If the homeless who need shelter or specialized living situations are also mentally ill, substance abusers, or multiproblem families, the NIMBY response can be vehement! The concern for the safety of those in the neighborhood, if "those people" are allowed to move in, can trigger a reaction of fear based on rational and irrational thoughts. It is certainly easy to get caught up in fear about property values, the fear of people unlike ourselves, and the fear that if "those people" are allowed here, others "just like them" will follow.

If we are going to provide safe, sanitary places with specialized services for people who have special needs, then those facilities must be located somewhere. A growing number of people who put the needs of others before their own parochial interests is being known as the IMBY's—the "In-My-Backyard" group. These rare people believe that there is room for everyone in the neighborhood, whether they are middle-class families or individuals and families whose housing will be accompanied by special services to supply their needs.

My friend Jack White (executive director of the Coalition for the Homeless in the District of Columbia) has described how difficult it is for his organization to "do good" by trying to obtain the necessary zoning changes to permit them to rehabilitate old houses (where no one lives now because the houses are too run-down) into housing for the homeless who need housing which includes specialized services to meet their needs. He laments about the roadblocks and hurdles to turning a dilapidated house into a safe home for the homeless. It may actually cost more to gain zoning approval than to make the house livable! Zoning laws within reason should be changed to provide housing for homeless people, not to discourage it.

You can make a difference by learning the facts about the needs of homeless families and children and offering that kind of help right in your own community or neighborhood, wherever those needs can be met. Quite frankly, you may not win any neighborhood popularity contests for your efforts!

Another example of one person who has made a difference is Olga Osby. Olga began advocacy for homeless children as she was completing her second year's graduate education in social work at Howard University. Olga, in addition to working with me at Travelers Aid International in a field practicum, also worked at a local family shelter to supplement her family's support for her education.

Olga, a young black woman, is warm and caring. She

has been raised with a sound basis in Christian values, especially concern for others. You can't help liking Olga. She always looks at life from the positive side and is willing to put her energies where her Christian values are.

In the fall of 1988, Olga learned that a group of Washington attorneys was interested in tutoring homeless children as a means of helping the children to catch up and keep up in school. The group, however, needed someone to organize the effort within the shelter, to identify the children needing tutoring, to arrange the necessary transportation (there was no room for such help at the overcrowded shelter), and to encourage the children to participate. Olga seized upon this need and agreed to organize the tutoring project.

The first night of tutoring was a nightmare with all that could possibly go wrong! The city officials didn't really believe that Olga could find so many children to attend a tutoring night, so not enough buses were available to transport the children across town. That meant Olga had to choose between accompanying the first busload of kids to the tutoring site and introducing them to their tutors or staying behind with the increasingly active and noisy group of "left-behind" children. With far too many children and far too few adults to help with the coordination, Olga determined that this tutoring was going to proceed anyway, even if she had to do everything herself!

It did proceed. The children who showed up that night were thrilled to have the undivided attention of adults for awhile. They absolutely loved it! They told their friends, and soon it seemed everyone wanted tutoring and wanted to have someone special who would take a personal interest in them! Even children who were not going to school would attend tutoring!

There is considerable need for these children to have caregivers besides their parents or guardians. In situations where families are sometimes forced to live for a long time under crowded conditions, where they have little opportunity for recreation or going out, children lack a sense of permanence or stability. They can display symptoms of depression, anxiety, and developmental delay. What a positive influence a relationship with a stable, caring adult can make!

Olga and her tutoring attorneys have made a tremendous difference! Homeless children living in unhealthy, crowded conditions with parents stretched to the breaking point are finding a haven of adults who are role models, who care about them, who want to help them.

If Olga, a student who cares about others, can make a difference in the lives of homeless children, what about you? What can you do? How can you make a difference?

What do Homeless Families and Their Children Need?

Here are some needs of families and their children which may help you consider how you can do your part:

1. Housing
2. Enough income to afford housing
3. Food
4. Employment or employment training, job placement
5. Education
6. Child care
7. Health care
8. Recreation
9. Help with specific needs
10. Specialized services to meet specialized needs.

Photo Courtesy of Carl R. Resener

8

Where Can a Runaway Go?

Resener

Many runaways have a home to which they can return, but they are afraid to do so because they fear being abused and/or neglected. There are runaways who, because of the life-style and behavior they experienced while on the streets, are too ashamed to return home. Other runaways have received word that their family has been dissolved by divorce or a remarriage. In one situation I dealt with, the family had moved away, leaving no forwarding address, making it impossible for the runaway to return home.

When there is no home available, a runaway may end up continuing his life on the streets, hoping his journey will carry him to an appropriate place. However, such is not the case for many runaways.

Street Population

Many runaways, finding it impossible to return home, continue to live on the streets until adulthood. Then they simply assume a place in the ranks of the homeless population. Many adults who become mission and shelter residents entered street life in their early teens. Living for years according to the "code of the streets," many runaways do not feel comfortable in any other environment. Their habits, work codes, and friends seem to be unbreakable chains that keep them within the confines of the street. After years out there, there is often no desire to change. Few if any contacts are made to family members by the street person. Often, family reunions I have witnessed involving street people occur when the street person dies. After years of separation, somehow the living relatives gather together to provide some type of "decent" burial of a deceased street person. I have buried many street persons whose only home was the streets. I have listened to the life story of the deceased from his relatives, and at times I have really thought that his/her death was a blessing, having heard of the heartaches and sorrow that had sent the now deceased running away to the streets for the rest of his life.

I have on certain occasions stated in my eulogy to a deceased street person: "Rest, my dear friend. Father will abuse you no more—no more feelings of worthlessness, no more guilt or shame, no more searching for peace, joy, and happiness. Where you did not find a home, a father's love here on earth, you have gone where God is your Father, heaven is your home, where there will be no tears, abuse, sorrow, or heartache. This is one home you will not need to run from."

Mental Community

Recently, I visited a mental hospital where I noticed the familiar face of a person who had frequented the mission's Anchor Home program. I asked a nurse what the person was doing there and why he would not recognize me. She replied that my one-time resident of the mission suffered "a mental blackout" due to abusive use of drugs. "He's completely beside himself and probably will require the constant care of some mental hospital. No one wants him."

Like my one-time resident, many young people end up in mental wards, partly because they have no home, and if there were one, they might find it different because of mental and physical problems they would carry with them. Parents and relatives are reluctant to accept mentally disturbed persons into their homes for two reasons: they do not know how to care for such a person, and they want to protect the rest of the family from the unpredictable actions of the mentally ill young person.

Many parents strongly object to the young person's returning home. Even though my friend was in a mental hospital, it was only for a short evaluation period, and then he was released from the hospital, like many other nonviolent mental patients, to live on the streets. That is where he is today. The mental-health problem, deinstitutionalization, the release of nonviolent mental patients from the nation's mental hospitals—all make it impossible for a mentally impaired young person to obtain long-term treatment or custodial care to protect himself and others from his abnormal behavior. Unless such a young person becomes violent and becomes a threat to himself or to others, he will have to live the rest of his life on the streets without ever receiving appropriate treatment to overcome his impairment. Parents who assume that someone else will take care of their mentally impaired child when they will not, are in for the shock of their lives when they discover that the local mental hospitals turn their backs on their mentally ill child just as they did.

Deinstitutionalization should be sacrificed in favor of

some form of reinstitutionalization, where nonviolent mental incompetence is treated the same as we treat those with a violent ailment. No one with mental problems should be kept outside of our mental-health resources, away from provisions for treatment, so the mental illness can be corrected or at least controlled by environment, as well as by medicine. No person with mental problems, young or old, should be denied mental-health resources so he or she must live at the mercy of the community that understands little about those problems.

Jail

"When I couldn't return home, then I used the streets to make a living and ended up going to prison for three years." The speaker was a young man who spent time in prison for peddling drugs.

"I had no intention of ending up in prison when I left home. But when I realized I had no home to return to, I became one who preyed on the runaways for a source of my income."

It is ironic that the victim of street life may well become a drug pusher, a prostitute, or even a pimp, preying on the new arrivals. Alternative homes for young persons are often jail or prison. Street life strains the honesty and integrity of every young person and for obvious reasons, as I have pointed out, many young persons end up in jail and finally prison.

As many a young person has told me: "Look, man, I've got to look out for myself. My old man don't want me. My ma don't want me. I'm just taking care of myself." However, in so doing, many a young person lands in jail because in his own mind he alibis, *I am only do-*

ing to others what others did or tried to do to me. I have no doubt that on certain occasions young persons have deliberately committed crimes for the purpose of being sent to prison because they had no home. Many kids have confessed to me, "Jail's even better than the streets. At least there you have something to eat and someone to talk to."

Armed Services

I recently bade good-bye to a resident of Anchor Home who was leaving for the armed services. He enlisted in the Navy simply because he did not have a home to which he could return. After he had run away from home, stayed away for a year and a half, he returned, only to discover that his parents had divorced, each living separately and each unable or unwilling to add him to their overburdened lives. Not wanting to live on the streets again, he enlisted in the Navy, "hoping I'll make new friends and become a part of a 'family,' even though it's scattered around the world." The armed services can become home to homeless young people who qualify scholastically. Though the military can never be a replacement for home, it is far better than returning to the streets and certainly more promising.

Road Jobs

Many young people who do not or cannot return home end up in jobs that call for travel on the road—sales, carnivals, circuses, and the like. These are certainly viable options for a young person when it is impossible to return. Of course, these are not the best either. The main problem I have seen in the lives of "carneys" is their detachment from the mainstream of society. They must travel so much they never have a chance to settle down until they are so old or crippled they can no longer travel. Too, young people are often taken advantage of by unscrupulous carnival or circus managers who exploit the kids' willingness to work. This type of work comes under the heading of "hard labor."

The managers have also used the "magic" atmosphere of belonging to the carnival or circus to infect the runaway with "carney" fever to the extent he is willing to become a permanent member of the carnival or circus family.

I well remember one of my first experiences with a "carney," a young man who was with a carnival. The carnival came to Nashville for ten days. During that time the fellow was injured in an accident, making it impossible for him to perform his duties. The day the carnival left town he was abandoned at the mission, leaving him in Nashville. He moaned sadly as I was checking him into the mission, "I thought I was one of them. I didn't think they would leave town without me!"

Young people who become "carney kids" soon realize that in the carnival world, if they cannot keep up with the schedule, the show will leave them behind. Such shows do not have to worry about replacements, for management is aware there is a young person in the next town waiting to replace his home with a traveling circus or carnival. Like a retiring seaman who spent his life on the seas, returning to land he has no family or associates with whom to unite. So it is with the young person who replaces his home with the carnival or circus. Soon there may not be a place to go, no place to call home.

Marriage

Another alternative for young people when they are not able to return home is to marry another street kid and to create their own home. On the surface, this sounds noble and courageous. However, it smacks of Hollywood in that marriage for young people is often an escape from reality. Many marriages among street youth are merely rebounds from rejection either from the family or the community. Many such marriages are merely replacements of what the young person has lost from his or her own personal family. I have been asked to perform the marriage of several runaway couples. I turned them all down because I sensed that marriage to them was only a means of leaving the street. Each spouse was expecting the other to make up what was lost in their life, and the sad truth of the matter was that neither had the strength to be of much help to the other.

Street life offers no provisions for marriage. Often the conversation goes as follows: Bill comes to me and asks, "Brother Resener, Helen and I are going to be married in the next ten minutes, and we want you to marry us."

I respond, "Why do you want to get married?"

Helen often answers, "We want a home of our own."

I ask, "Where are you going to live?"

Bill replies, "Brother Resener, we thought we could live here at the mission until we can get on our feet."

I hurt deeply during these counseling sessions with runaways who honestly believe they can have some type of home on the streets. They want a home to replace the one that has been dissolved through personal problems. They want to experience that "sense of belonging to someone" to the point they are willing to marry another runaway, believing each has the same goals and that each can become the role model that a successful family requires.

Of course, I am not the only preacher on "skid row," so when I tell a couple I do not believe that marriage at this time is the answer to their situation, they hurry off to another minister who thinks that their desire to be married is "heaven-sent"—so he marries them. Several hours after the wedding or the following morning, the newly married couple returns to me and announces, "Well, preacher, we got married, and we want to stay at the mission."

It is usually not long before each spouse realizes that the other cannot fill the needs they thought marriage would provide. Bill could not land a job or provide Helen with a home except the city shelter. Usually having no car, they are on the streets constantly, never really alone. Soon, Helen comes to me and wails, "Bill is just like my father. He drinks and beats me up. I can't stand it any longer."

Later, Bill arrives and spins his story of Helen's inadequacies. Unfortunately, the marriage of Bill and Helen becomes a repeat of the outcome of their own families. A runaway situation does not offer a satisfactory courtship that a successful marriage requires. It is usually an adverse experience for those runaways who believe otherwise.

Ward of the Department of Human Services

When asked about returning home, a teenager replied, "I can't go home because I'm in the custody of the Department of Human Services." When asked why he was in a shelter for young men, he explained, "I ran away from the home DHS placed me in." Court-ordered foster homes do not always work. When I, along with Judy Hall, walked the streets of New York, we were informed by social workers in the youth shelters that a very large number, nearly 60 percent, of young people living on the streets were runaways from the foster-care system.

Reverend Leonard Nabors, who supervises the Anchor Home for Young Men in Nashville, meets foster-home runaways quite frequently. From his counseling sessions and involvement with the foster-care program in Nashville and the nation, Leonard speaks openly and candidly regarding the foster-care program as it applies to these teenagers:

> As I see young men come into the Anchor Home from foster-parent or group-home settings, I realize there can never be a place that may meet the needs of a real home, a home where parents and siblings work together to achieve a common goal.
>
> Many of the young men I have seen coming from the foster-care programs are very apprehensive of any change, whether coming into a new foster-care setting or any type of court-ordered, foster-care program. With this apprehension come distrust, rebellion, or even hatred. The young person may feel betrayed because he or she has been lied to and "jerked around" so much that they really do not know what or who to believe anymore. So they are unwilling to believe anyone. They even reach a point of believing that no one cares about them, resulting in an "I-don't-care" frame of mind. At this point they either run away, turn to drugs, or desire suicide—anything for an escape from rejection. For they do feel rejected, worthless, and hopeless.

This is why I feel Anchor Home is being utilized by our local Department of Human Services. The young men escorted here by DHS counselors are shown love and caring in a Christ-centered environment, not only by the staff but also by the other residents as well. We become a family, living together, working together, playing together, and going to church together. Those who come to Anchor Home rebellious, rude, and afraid to drop the shield they have built around themselves to protect themselves from any future hurt, must first be shown respect, sternness, fairness, and genuine love before they are willing to drop that shield. They are virtually incapable of loving or caring about another person when they first enter the home. They do not understand the rules, even though they are clearly written out for them to read. They do not comprehend how to live with others where everything is shared equally.

Part of the confusion of living with others—sharing and caring for others—is because in some foster-care programs there are no written rules. Kids must learn by trial and error, thus causing undue pain for both parties. Another problem of some foster-care programs is the lack of demand for consistency of behavior. Each person in the home must obey the rules of living together and must realize that the penalty for breaking a rule will be dealt with without partiality. However, each person disciplined for disrupting the program with his misbehavior should be disciplined in love. He must be shown that, even in discipline, the welfare of the individual, not the rule, is the main concern.

My conclusion is that too many foster-care programs lack love, the kind of love that is caring and consistent. Those programs may lack guidelines that will help the young person to understand from the start what is expected of him. They may also lack unity of purpose that enables the young person to see that the program can mean something to him today as well as tomorrow. Unfortunately, foster-care programs sometimes lack cohesiveness whereby the residents feel as though they belong to a family, rather than to a group of disoriented individuals, using one another to grab the biggest piece of the pie. It is understandable why a person in such a foster-care environment can become rebellious, rude, uncaring for others as well as himself, and run away to the streets. Here at Anchor Home we try to create a "unique home atmosphere" where each resident can actually be treated as a family member.

Cults

When a young person has no home he may unite with a cult and be willing to accept a quasi-religious order as a replacement for a family. A young man, when asked why he joined a cult, stated, "They made me feel like I was somebody important." Dr. Ahmad Ardekani, a St. Louis psychiatrist, wrote, "In some cases, you have a highly intelligent teenager who is just curious about the occult." Ardekani continued: "But more often we're talking about teenagers who are poorly self-adjusted, suffering from low self-esteem, bored, somewhat rebellious and desperately wanting to belong to a peer group."[1] As we understand the phenomenon of kids who have been abused, neglected, rejected, and have become rebellious, it becomes quite clear how kids on the street would latch onto a cultic group as an attractive replacement for a family, at least until they advance into the deeper meaning, motives, and methods required to become a full member of the cult family. At that time, when total commitment to the cult is demanded, the young person's grandiose ideas of belonging to a "family" may become shattered by the demands of the cult until he is once more in the center of threats, terror, and even physical abuse.

In most religious cults, there are four major areas which not only attract a searching, yearning street kid, but also hold the newcomer to the group. Often the young person finds himself involved in activities he never dreamed existed. In most of these groups there is a strong emphasis on:

Deliverance.—The cult leaders work the streets and locate young people who are having difficulty surviving. Cult devotees take advantage of these situations, promising the young recruit the necessities of life. The street kid accepts the promises of relief and goes with the workers. The fact that the group helped the young person when he was down and out is used to create an affection and an attachment to the cult. "After all," the cult leader can say to a young street person, "we were there when you needed somebody." The group works heavily on the conscience of a young candidate, convincing him that they brought life and meaning to him. It is easy for the young person to testify, "Hey, these are nice guys."

Deception.—The second major area of the cult group is deception through its educational activities. The young recruit must be indoctrinated in the teachings of the group. Hours and hours must be spent reading and studying the basic beliefs of the group, as well as the purposes of its existence. In this area the young recruit may become somewhat concerned about the cult's expectations and requirements. Brainwashing best explains what the young recruit experiences. Only those who cannot be "brainwashed" into believing and accepting the full teachings of the cult will have a tough time remaining in the group.

Devotion.—The third area of importance in the cult is the devotion to its particular teachings, procedures, and rituals. Tests of the young recruit's sincerity can range from being willing to work long, hard hours on behalf of the organization, such as selling flowers in public places, working in stores without wages, laboring on farms, bringing food into the headquarters. Other tests of devotion, especially in satanic cults, may call for the killing of animals and, in some instances, the killing of human beings! If a young recruit is leery of his involvement in the cult, by the time he finishes his indoctrination, the demanded proofs of devotion will make him more aware of what is being required of him to be a part of the "family"—a surrender of his whole life to a cult leader. Each year in the state of Tennessee hundreds of runaway children become involved in satanic religious groups, including some of the most gruesome, sadistic ceremonies.

Discipline.—The fourth significant characteristic of a cult preying upon the street kids is that of discipline. These cults are strict disciplinarians in breaking the spirit as well as the body of the young trainee. What a recruit is asked to believe, as well as what is expected of him regarding his behavior, demands a rigid, strict outlook on life. The matter of self-denial is of the most importance. To deny self in order to make the cult effective in its purposes is to demonstrate the greatest respect for the group. Giving one's life for the sake of the organization is not beyond the realm of possibility.

Escapees from such groups have told me they fear for their lives because of their departure from the group. Fear of being disciplined for departing a cult devastates those who have broken away. The Nashville Union Mission has provided refuge from such retaliation by the leaders of cults. Those who flee such groups fear not only physical harm but satanic influence which they believe can penetrate even the walls of the buildings to punish them. There is no doubt in my mind that many of the street kids who become involved in these groups end up in our state mental hospitals, state prisons, and, worst of all, some end up in unmarked graves in a public cemetery.

Suicide

The biblical account of the prodigal son is the story of a runaway boy who spent his inheritance on "riotous" living. Sitting in a pigpen, he realized his pitiful situation and reasoned, *I could go back home and take my place as a servant.* So he returned home. However, the father received him as his son, not as a servant, and restored him to his former position within the family. Many runaways today cannot go back to such a home; they have no such father or mother waiting to receive them.

As a result, they often feel their alternative is suicide. Each year, thousands of young runaways are laid to rest in some obscure part of a cemetery. They take their lives rather than continue living on the streets. Several times each year at Anchor Home, a young man will attempt to snuff out his own life. Sad to admit, some succeed.

When asked, "Why did you try to end your life?" the reply will generally be, "I didn't want to be a bother to anyone" or "I didn't think I had anything left to live for." One fellow answered, "I just wanted to end the hurt." In my opinion the highest percentage of suicide among the homeless population is among runaway youth. It is horrible that life is so bleak and cruel for many of our nation's youth that they desire death over life. Surely we can offer them a better alternative.

In conclusion, where do kids go when they do not have a home to return to? They do not disappear from the face of the earth. They do not simply fade away. They are somewhere, and they, for the most part, are not writing to someone a postcard with the message, "Having a great time. Wish you were here."

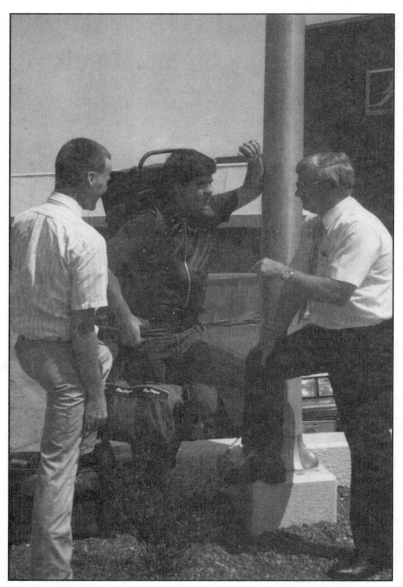

Photo Courtesy of Carl R. Resener

9

Getting Johnny Off the Streets

Resener

If and when a parent wants his runaway child back home, he has several options.

By force

The parents search for the runaway son or daughter until they find him or her and, if the child is a juvenile, they can have him or her arrested and forcibly brought back home, whether the runaway child is willing or not. Positively speaking, using force to make the runaway return gets the child off the streets and puts the destructive elements of street life in check, at least for the time being. Perhaps the runaway will not experience more harm than what has already been done. In some measure, the parent shows love and concern for the runaway, whether or not the runaway accepts it. The negative side of using force is that it may kindle more rebellion and resistance.

A family was driving to the country. The child in the backseat was jumping up and down, trying to crawl from the back to the front seat to reach mother's lap. The father kept commanding the child to sit down. The child would not mind, so the father yelled, "Sit down or I'll stop this car and take you outside and whip you."

Quickly, the child obeyed. However, as the child sat brooding over having to sit down, he coldly protested, "Daddy, I'm sitting down, but in my mind I'm standing up." A major risk in forcing the runaway to return home is that the runaway will either say and/or think, "Daddy, I'm home, but in my mind I'm still running."

If the runaway is coerced into coming home, the condition of the home life-style will be the determining factor of how long the runaway will remain there. If home conditions are still as they were, a condition which initiated the departure, the runaway—though back home—will leave his belongings packed up and ready to go again, at least mentally.

By waiting

Parents can play the waiting game with their runaway. That is, they can bide time until the runaway gets so tired, hungry, lonely, and frustrated that he or she will call home for help to come back. On the surface this is what most parents hope for. In theory, the parent thinks, *When he sees what the world is all about, he'll come back home.* In fact, a large number of runaways return home within twenty-four hours of their departure.

The waiting game, however, is risky as well as demoralizing to the runaway. Waiting may "telegraph" to the runaway that perhaps the parents really don't care for him after all. I have talked to runaways who confessed, "I ran away to get my parents' attention. They lived in their world so much that they had no time for me. I ran away so maybe they would come after me." A young girl sobbed, "My parents didn't care enough to come after me to see what was wrong."

The waiting game can produce the wrong results in

that, instead of the runaway's coming home, they may run further away from home because of what seems to be parental acceptance that their child is gone. I have been told by parents of the returning child that their waiting to locate and bring back their child actually demoralized him. Waiting for the runaway to return on his or her own because of trouble encountered on the streets can create defeatism and hopelessness within the returnee.

Though he is home, the runaway will feel that parents are smirking because he can't run away and make it on his own. The parents may have him home, but he may feel his situation is still hopeless. His running away didn't accomplish anything that would change his home situation. So, he or she will consider himself or herself hopelessly locked in a situation there is no use trying to change.

I am afraid some parents use the waiting game in hopes of "breaking the will" of the kid. The results are disastrous. The runaway may be "broken" of physically running away, but he may easily "run away" through drugs, alcohol, and other destructive habits.

Another cruel side to the waiting game is that—and I also know this from my experiences dealing with runaways here at the mission—every minute a runaway is away from home he is exposed to constant threats to his survival. Many young people die violent deaths. Yes, the waiting game is extremely risky. I recall a father who cried to me, "We just now found her grave. We waited too long to begin our search for her."

By asking

Several times a year we receive circulars sent out by families of runaways. We are asked to have them on our bulletin board at each of the mission's facilities. The circular will generally state, "Johnny [name of the runaway], please come home. Please call collect. We love you. Mom and Dad." Several times a year members of runaways' families will come to Nashville and search the city for their loved ones. I have been involved in several reunions between families and their runaways.

After general greetings, with hugs and kisses normally initiated by the parents, the runaway is asked to return home with them. The expected happy scene changes into a somewhat serious business meeting. The runaway replies to the thought of returning home with solemn, serious questions, "Why should I return?" "Do you want to beat me again?" or "What's in it for you if I do come back?"

I have thought in the past, *How cruel to talk to your parents like that!* But having a deeper understanding about the reasons why young people run away from home, I try not to criticize such remarks, because the runaway assuredly knows the home situation far better than I ever could.

Parents must keep their motives up front when they ask a child to come back. They must make sure they are not asking selfishly, except for the fact that they do not want their child to be hurt by living in a deplorable setting. The runaway will test those motives to figure out if the parents want him home mainly to avoid the embarrassment of having a runaway child or are suffering financial loss by attempting to keep up with him. One concern is sure—the returnee will want to know, "Do you want me back enough to change some things that sent me away, such as physical and sexual abuse, neglect, or drugs?"

When parents ask the child to return, they are obligated to listen and accept changes the runaway feels necessary to assure a safe and secure return. I have heard young people say, "No, I won't come back. Even if you take me by force. I'll run away again. You haven't changed." I have also heard fathers lay down the law to their runaway, "I want you back, but it is going to be under my conditions." There have been situations where I really thought there would be a family reunion in my office only to see pride and self-will build such a wall between parents and their runaway that both parties left with no desire for a reunion. No parents should ask a runaway to return unless they are willing to accept certain changes in the life-style of the home.

By adjusting

Some of the most promising reunions I have seen were when parents have taken the initiative and admitted to the runaway, "We all have made some mistakes in our home, and as a family we should be willing and able to work them out." A reunion in which each side can admit they are part of the problem will continue after the family is home. You feel a reunion is real when a father will confess, "Son, I didn't realize I was hurting you."

By prayer

I have no doubt that prayer has reunited many sons and daughters. To be forced back home by parents and to be led back home by the parents' prayers are two different approaches. The runaway returned by force is humiliated by his inability to be a successful runaway. In his own mind, he returns home as a captive. The kid who left a good home because of some selfish, self-motivated purpose often realizes that his conscience will not permit him to continue his sojourn away from home. Like the prodigal son in the Bible (Luke 15), he sizes up the deplorable situation he has helped create and reasons that it is best to return home and ask for his parents' forgiveness. Arriving home, the "prodigal" is received into the eager arms of his parents, who rejoice that God has answered their prayers.

Throughout my many years at the mission, I have come to this conclusion regarding parents looking for their runaways: the non-Christian parent can use only the visible means of searching and locating the wandering loved one. Parents often succumb to the pressure and anxiety of looking for their kids. They may have the same concern and intent for their runaway child, but so often the outcome is far different from that of a Christian home. Yes, Christian homes do experience the runaway problem. However, the Christian has one resource that not even the runaway realizes: prayer. Prayer does not eliminate the efforts of searching, locating, and traveling to find the runaways, but through prayer the search is easier and more productive.

I cannot count the times when I or one of the staff has called the parents of a runaway and heard them almost yell into the phone, "Thank God. He has answered our prayers!" Many a runaway has told me, "I don't know how I ended up in Nashville," only to learn that his parents had an entire community praying for him. Many a runaway has come to the mission convicted in his heart by God to go home because of the prayers of folks back home. The difference is: when God is involved in the runaway's return, the entire family is moved to effect whatever changes are necessary. The impact of prayer not only can change the direction of the runaway, but can also change the lives of the pray-ers, so adjustments within the home are easily and eagerly made to resolve all or most differences.

Since I have mediated numerous family reunions, I have sensed a threefold need among returnees. One or all of these needs always comes up in the discussion between the parent and the runaway. These needs had something to do with the initial act of running away and are basic requirements to be resolved before the runaway feels that it is all right to return home.

The Need to Belong

Many runaways simply explain that they ran away from home because they no longer felt they were part of the family. They were crowded out by bad times their families were experiencing such as drug problems and financial matters. Other young runaways contend their parents were so ambitious to climb the ladder of success that they emotionally blocked their own child out of their lives.

Other kids sensed they were replaced by "new members" of the family from a new marriage which added more children to the existing family. For a young person to see a "new kid" in Daddy's arms or in Mother's lap— to view a "stranger" getting the attention he used to receive—is demoralizing. Sometimes the "veteran" sibling senses that maybe he is not wanted, so he prepares to "get out of the way" by leaving home.

Many times the parents do not realize they have excluded one—or perhaps all—of their children until one of them runs away. A familiar request from the runaway to the parent, as they seek a reunion, will always include something about family participation, thus assuring the returning runaway a meaningful place in the family structure. The prodigal son knew he could go home and become a farmhand for his father. How surprised he was when the father exulted, "You are my son—not my servant!" This is the type of "belonging" today's runaway needs upon returning home.

The Need for Importance

A young person must feel he or she is more than a meal ticket through the food-stamp program, more than a physical replacement for a father who isn't satisfied sexually by his wife, more than a punching bag upon which the parent may vent his frustration.

> "My parents say I'm crazy to stay away from home because if I'd stayed home I'd probably have my own car by now," states Marie, a young woman who ran away because of being abused by her stepfather. "But what's a car worth if your parents don't think you're worth anything?"[1]

> Working with the youth of the inner city we see hundreds of young people who have poor self-images, who are constantly told they are "ugly" people. We must demonstrate to our young people that they are of great worth. If our young people do not feel positive about themselves, if they do not have a good self-image, they cannot excel academically, emotionally or spiritually.[2]

Long before the runaway hits the streets he had severe problems of self-esteem and self-worth. How much self-esteem can a young woman have after being sexually violated by her father, uncle, or friend of the family? How important can a young man feel about himself when his parents leave him in the hands of strangers for a "night out" or a business trip? No wonder when he runs away and the parents discuss "reunion," the kid wants to know where he stands on the parents' list of priorities.

The Need for Security

As the potential runaway grew into childhood, he took it for granted that his parents would provide for him and protect him from himself as well as from others. However, as he became aware of incidents and events in his life maybe he realized that his parents or guardians were hardly protecting him at all. In fact, the parents themselves, as well as others, were perhaps involved directly and indirectly in the incidents which caused him pain physically, morally, and/or mentally. The kid soon found himself with no one to talk to, no one to trust in his own family, so he escaped from the very place which once seemed to be the safest place in all the world.

When the parents catch up with their runaway son or daughter, the security issue is always discussed at length. Many of the runaways who left home because of physical and sexual abuse have reason to believe that the parents will not protect them from future incidents. In fact, according to Ruth C. Blanche, director of the Center for the Study of Human Sexuality at Montclair State College:

> Parents sometimes don't believe the runaway's accusations about being abused by a relative of the family or if the runaway was abused. The parents will state that the child must have asked for it. Parents who learn of their child's victimization are also victims and may want to strike out at the child.

Parents who are looking for their runaway should not do so with the idea of giving him a "second chance," except where the situation is a willfully rebellious one. Then parents may show the runaway a gracious and generous attitude.

In too many situations the runaway has the right to complain, "Look, Folks, I gave you a chance at first. I trusted you, but you allowed or caused me to be hurt in many different ways. I must decide if I should give *you* a second chance." In my opinion, the runaway is in the driver's seat when deciding if there is going to be a re-union. Too often the parents want to emerge from a runaway situation looking good. However, the history of runaways shows that this is not the case. For too long, the runaway has been forced to accept the pain of abuse and neglect, as well as the shame of being a runaway.

In defense, a parent may say to me, "Aren't you buying the story of the runaway more than you should?" My reply is, "Perhaps." In some instances, the story of home is blown out of proportion, but overall I tend to believe the stories coming from the runaway as true. A parent may retort, "Look at my runaway child, dirty, drugged, sexed half to death, and so forth. That is not the child I raised!" I quickly reply that this child is not the same person who left home.

What we see are the results of running away. A parent may not be responsible for what happens to a young person on the street, but they may be responsible for the reasons why the young person is there. Life is too cruel on the street for a runaway to be playing games with his or her parents, although a small percentage of runaways admit to this. What the runaway goes through on the streets informs me that there is more than a "little misunderstanding" in numerous homes.

A home in which each child has a sense of belonging, importance, and no reason to fear is one that no mentally healthy child would ever want to leave.

Photo Courtesy of Carl R. Resener

10

Christian Parents—Prodigal Children

Resener

> "Train up a child in the way he should go; and when he is old, he will not depart from it" (Prov. 22:6).

Parents have used this verse as the Golden Rule of child rearing. If a child turns out to be a successful Christian, the parents can look with pride at the verse. However, if the child turns out to be a secular person, void of any spiritual standards in his life, then the parents would use the verse for self-condemnation and consider themselves parental failures.

The verse certainly emphasizes parental responsibility which I believe most Christian parents are willing to express to the child. However, I do not accept the fact that the verse is a written guarantee that nowhere in the child's upbringing will there be rebellion against the restraints placed upon the child as a means of training. The fact that a young person rebels against discipline does not mean that the parent failed as much as it reveals that some lessons in life are not going to be accepted until the young person sees for himself, through personal failure, the results of breaking those guidelines the parents placed on him.

Not all training is accomplished without a test by the

young person to see if the restraint is acceptable. A restraint is only acceptable when the young person regards it as a positive or negative benefit for him to possess as a way of life. This means that the young person may go against the parents' wishes simply to test the principle for himself. This may imply that the young person may not trust the advice of the parent or it may mean that he must learn it for himself, in spite of the parents' counsel and instruction in the training period of a child's life.

Blessed is the home that produces children who do not go against the restraints of their parents. However, the Bible offers hope and help for the parents who have had a son or a daughter depart from the home to test the restraints or even to flee from parental guidance. Instead of condemnation, God's Word gives guidance and assurance that the runaway may well end up following God's Word as a result of running away. The young person was having a very difficult time doing that at home.

Charles H. Spurgeon, pastor of the Metropolitan Temple in London, England, in the 1800s, had these encouraging words for Christian parents who are experiencing the trauma of a runaway child.

> Now I want to speak to some of you Christian people about the matter of runaways. Have you a son who has left home? Is he a willful, wayward young man who has gone away because he could not bear the restraints of a Christian home? It is a sad thing. It should be so—a very sad thing, but do not despond or even have a thought of despair about him.
>
> You do not know where he is, but God does; and you cannot follow him, but the Spirit of God can. He is going on a voyage to Shanghai. Ah, there may be a Paul at Shanghai who is to be the means of his salvation (as in the case of the runaway slave Onesimus recorded in the

Book of Philemon in the New Testament of the Holy Scriptures), and as that Paul is not in England, your son must go there. Is it to Australia that he is going? There may be a word spoken there by the blessing of God to your son which is the only word which will ever reach him.

I cannot speak it; nobody in London can speak it; but the man there will; and God, therefore, is letting him go away in all of his willfulness and folly that he may be brought under the means of grace which will prove effectual to his salvation. The worst thing that can happen to a young man is sometimes the best thing that can happen to him, especially if it results in his conversion to Christ.

Look at the runaway in the light of earnest, active benevolence, and rouse yourselves to conquer it. Our duty is to hope on and pray on. It may be, perhaps, that he is departed for a season, that thou shouldst receive him forever! Perhaps the boy has been wayward that his sin may come to a crisis and a new heart may be given him. Perhaps your daughter's evil has been developed that now the Lord has convinced her of sin and bearing her to the Saviour's feet. At any rate, if the case be ever so bad, hope in God and pray on.[1]

David, King of Israel, had a son named Absalom who surely broke David's heart as did other sons of certain Bible greats. Christian parents today must be aware that their hearts can be broken by a runaway son or daughter. As parents we must be as prepared as possible to meet a runaway crisis in the home. Barbara Baumgardner, mother of three as well as a free-lance writer, suggests the following guidelines for Christian parents of a runaway:

1. *Face the truth.*—Fear often stops when we have the courage to run toward the giant that is scaring us,

just as David ran toward the giant Goliath (1 Sam. 17). If we suspect that our teenager is involved in an unhealthy relationship, we need to ask him or her about it. Don't berate, criticize, or show disapproval of a child in trouble. He or she needs a noncondemning parent with whom to talk. Like Job stated, "Shall we indeed accept good from God and not accept adversity?" (Job 2:10, NASB). Sometimes a family meeting will allow family members to express feelings of injustice and hurt. It takes courage for us to hear the truth from those we love, but it is not so frightening as hearing that we have been unapproachable.

2. Try to see the situation through your son's or daughter's eyes.—The hardest thing for children to do is admit that they have disappointed us. It is difficult to call home and say, "I was wrong to run away and I want to come home."

3. Prayer is essential.—God's Word says, "Be anxious for nothing, but in everything by prayer and supplication with thanksgiving let your requests be known to God" (Phil. 4:6, NASB). In other words, trust, be thankful that God is there, and pray. Pray for God's protection for your child, using Psalm 91:10-11 as a guideline. Anticipate the blessing that is to come.

4. Recognize that there is a point of release.—A time may come when we need to free ourselves from our child for a while, otherwise he or she will break our hearts daily. "There was that moment," one mother explained, "when I knew I had to be more than a mother. I needed to be a friend who would be there to love and support her." Second Timothy 1:7 and John 14:27 should also be considered.

5. Relinquish over and over.—Sometimes the road to

restoration must be paved with relinquishment and forgiveness (Phil. 3:13). Christian families are not immune to crisis, but those who arm themselves with knowledge and love will have a better rate of survival.[2]

As director of the Nashville Union Mission, I have received many interesting phone calls. I remember a call from a mother whose runaway son had ended up at our mission. She stated that during his time at the mission he had not only heard the challenge to "straighten out one's life and return home and begin to live responsibly," which is the constant message given to young and old, but he accepted the challenge, came home, and had become an active member of the family once more. She pointed out that from the day the young man left home she prayed he would meet someone who would give him some good advice about what he should do with his life. She continued, "God answered my prayers when he ended up at your place."

David said, "Before I was afflicted I went astray" (Ps. 119:67). Sometimes God uses street life as a means of afflicting a prodigal son or daughter so the experiences of living on the streets become a "schoolmaster," quickly educating the runaway that "there's no place like home," especially a Christian home.

I believe it should be noted that there are many good organizations and individuals who help the homeless and runaways to return home—rescue missions in particular. I have always considered the Nashville Union Mission as a "Jonah's whale." Only when Jonah was swallowed up by the whale did he reconsider God's will for his life and resolved, if God would place him back into "the land of the living," especially on dry ground, he would carry out the task God had initially called on him to fulfill. A rescue mission is not the best place for a runaway to end his journey away from home. It is, however, the best place to end up when there are dedicated workers to encourage the young person to return home, if at all possible. Parents should, as they pray for their wandering loved ones, also pray for the "Jonah's whales" across the country that most likely will be at least a stopping-off place for the young prodigal.

The following letter was received by Reverend Leonard Nabors, whose young men's program I have already mentioned, from a young man he helped to go home:

Dear Rev. Nabors,

Just a few lines to let you know I made it home, and I would not have done it without you and Brother Martin's guiding hands. I have become a full-fledged truck driver.

Well, Rev. Nabors, Merry Christmas to you and all of the young men at Anchor Home. God bless you, for you did me a great justice when I needed your help. Had it not been for you I would still be a wanderer, or worse—a street person.

What Parents Could Have Done

The following article is from the pen of Fred Green, juvenile probation officer, Galveston, Texas. These are actual interviews with teens headed to "reform school." Answers stem from the question, "What could your parents have done to help you?"

1. "Keep Your Cool." Do not lose your head in every crisis. Kids need confidence and a steady hand around. Keep your soul settled.

2. "Do not get hung up on a job that keeps you away from home." Fathers, keep in touch with your kids somehow. Mothers, cut the heavy social schedule so you can be home to supervise the children.

3. "Do not get strung out." Stay away from liquor and sleeping pills. Be normal. Be "square."

4. "Bug me a little." Use strict, loving discipline. Show the kids who is boss. They want it this way. Do not just let them ride out a storm. Give them an anchor.

5. "Do not blow your class." Keep the dignity of parenthood. Stay on the pedestal your kids have put you on. Do not dress, act, or "swing" like the teens do.

6. "Light me a candle." Show your children the way to faith. Give them the security of a living faith.

7. "Take the world off my shoulders." Share your kids' problems. Talk about morals, life, love, eternity, beauty, peace of mind, and values with them. Help them believe the world is a good place in which to live.

8. "Shake me up." Punish me when I first go wrong. Tell my why. Convince me that more severe measures will come if I transgress again in the same manner. Do not punish me just in anger, though.

9. "Call my bluff." Stand firm on what is right, even when your kid threatens to run away or become a delinquent, or drop out of school. Stay in there with him, and the bluffing will cease in 98 percent of the cases.

10. "Be honest with me." All the time, tell the truth. Praise when you can; criticize when you must. But never keep your children in doubt where you stand on important matters.

For you parents who have children still living at home, it is not too late to start practicing all that is mentioned above!

11

A Message for Religious Bodies

Hall

In this book we have cited the examples of many servant churches in this country who are reaching out to homeless individuals and families in a spirit of love and compassion. These churches exemplify the words of Jesus,

> For I was hungry, and you gave Me something to eat; I was thirsty, and you gave Me drink; I was a stranger and you invited Me in; naked, and you clothed Me; I was sick, and you visited Me; I was in prison and you came to Me (Matt. 25:35-36 NASB).

We want to encourage pastors and congregations to become involved in social issues, to care about what happens in our communities, and to become active and productive in developing answers to some of these troubling questions. How can we sit back and depend solely upon social-service agencies to have all the answers? Can't we see gaps in the services our communities provide, gaps the church should fill? Can we turn our faith into action to address increasing homelessness?

In downtown Washington, D.C., the congregation at Luther Place Lutheran Church has opened a regular soup kitchen to feed the many hungry and homeless

159

Dr. Carl R. Resener

Dr. Judy Hall

people in the neighborhood. In addition, the church has rehabilitated nearby property to provide transitional housing for the homeless. Even when zoning restrictions of the city favored keeping buildings boarded up rather than made livable to the homeless, the church spoke out. Finally, the city relented, and the church moved on with its mission of turning its faith into action on behalf of "the least of these."

Other churches team up with missions or other organizations which help the homeless. This makes it possible for suburban churches in more affluent communities to have a direct connection with homeless services. Food and clothing can be collected from churches throughout a community and distributed from several central locations accessible to the homeless. Church members can volunteer to tutor homeless individuals in those skills which will enable them to gain a high-school diploma, qualify for employment, or even to fill out applications for welfare benefits.

Pastors play a pivotal role in helping congregations become aware of the needs of homeless individuals and families in the community, organizing congregations to assist the homeless and cooperating with other churches or community organizations on behalf of the homeless. Pastors can also speak out about the problems of the homeless and advocate improved services, so churches can become strategic solvers of this growing problem.

In other chapters we have discussed what we have seen all over this nation. We have walked the streets where homeless people eke out an existence. We have talked with homeless families and their children as they struggle to survive under conditions which are intolerable! We have discussed the problem with social workers and other service workers who spend every working day (and even non-working days) trying to help homeless families and youth. We have witnessed tears of desperation by the homeless as well as tears of frustration by those trying to help them.

As we have escorted you on this walk through homelessness, we have told you about the countless men, women, and children who make up the homeless in the United States. Their stories are as different as the homeless are. Yet there is a common theme to their stories. Parents want jobs and a stable place to live and to raise their children. Even when those parents have serious problems which interfere with their ability to be self-sufficient, they still have the same dream.

We have also written about examples of individuals who have made and are making a difference in the lives of homeless youth and families. Most of these examples are ordinary people who put their faith into action. They didn't wait for someone else to be the first to organize a response to the problem. They declared, in the words of Isaiah, "Here am I, send me," and they began to move into action about the problem. Not waiting until all the answers were neatly in place or until the community was fully organized for action, these individuals faced a pressing problem and began, without fanfare, to do something about it. They became organizers, advocates, and Christians who reached out to others, even those who were seemingly "unworthy." They reached out to children, youth, parents, and single individuals in many different strategies. But they all reached out in an effort to make a difference. And they all believed what they would do could make a vast difference. What about you? What kind of problem do you identify in your community? What kind of difference can *you* make?

A Message for Religious Bodies

Jesus said, "And the King will answer and say to them, 'Truly I say to you, to the extent that you did it to one of these brothers of Mine, even the least of them, you did it to Me'" (Matt. 25:40, NASB).

Epilogue

Resener

Reaction

It is not enough to write a book covering kids on the street. We must not only discover the reasons that make children, voluntarily or non-voluntarily, depart from their homes, *but* develop attitudes and actions that will prevent the abused, wasted lives of America's children. We must rediscover the sanctity of childhood. To achieve this we must do the following:

We must dramatize the fact that young people live in terror and under the threat of constant violence.

The American poet John Bishop Peale wrote, "The most tragic thing about the war was not that it made so many dead men, but that it destroyed the tragedy of death."[1] The abuse of children, as we see in our day, does not seem to bother us as a nation as much as the benefits we lose when children are no longer available to do our bidding. A mother may well regret the reduction of food stamps and welfare benefits over regretting that the child has run away or has died through physical abuse. A father may be angry regarding his runaway daughter or son because he is no longer able to satisfy his lust but may care little about what may happen to the young person who had to leave the confines of their home.

"Families are throwing children out of their homes long before the youth are ready to leave," concluded a United States Senate committee. "When they try to return, youngsters often find door locks changed and telephones slammed down by parents who are not willing or able to cope with them."

The U.S. National Network of Runaway and Youth Services states that the number of homeless and runaway children in the U.S. alone ranges from 1.3 million to 2 million each year. Experts estimate that between one-third and one-half of those youngsters are thrown out of their homes by their parents.[2]

We must *criticize* the system that *creates* problems rather than solutions. "The critical issue is not left-wing or right-wing; it is the moral center. How we treat children in the dawn of life and how we treat old people in the sunset of life are measures of our character."[3]

We have come to the point in American life where we place legality above the ethical. In fact, we have made such acts as abortion, pornography, and homosexuality legal through our court systems, regardless of the question of ethics. We have exposed the children of the land to threats which have been made legal for the adult world to perpetuate upon children. Through many court systems, abortion is an acceptable means of getting rid of an unwanted baby. Through many court systems, lesbians and gays can have custody of a child in a divorce case where the spouse divorces because of lesbianism or homosexuality. Through the system a mother can be jailed for hiding her child from the father who is known to be a child abuser.

Criticism must be levied against the system which rules in favor of those who find it easy to abuse physically and mentally ill children. Courts today leave the child unprotected from the darker desires of the adult world. We must criticize the system that totally ignores those who would be affected negatively by the laws passed by government. Our leaders must be as concerned over preventing child abuse as they are about the voting practices of the adult population.

We must analyze the loss of a young person— mentally, physically, and spiritually. This book is written on the theory of the sanctity of human life, most especially a child's life *before and after* its entry into the world. Therefore, whatever can happen to a child that will prevent its entrance into the world or contribute to the child's inability to enjoy a full-grown personality must be considered and treated as an enemy to the child. It must be perceived that the loss of a child, mentally and physically, is life's severest loss.

A child who is lost is *irreplaceable*. However a child is lost, that young, precious life can never be replaced. Each life conceived is unique and distinct in personality, unique in features and characteristics. If something happens to hinder that child from achieving maturity, that distinct individual is lost from the human race. Because of physical or mental abuse, though, many children will emerge into the world that can never replace those who were not permitted to do so simply because someone determined that they should not have a chance to become involved in the affairs of life.

The loss of a child is *irreversible*. In many situations where a child has suffered extreme physical or mental abuse, there is no cure. We need to realize children do not grow out of being mistreated physically, sexually, or mentally. Once a child has been violated physically or sexually the results are a lifetime reaction, causing serious emotional and life-style behavior. Children are never too young to realize that they have been violated, and they never live long enough to the extent those awful acts they experience do not affect life, meaning relationships with those around them. Those who perpetuate abuse on little children on the premise that the child is too young to remember need only to visit mental institutions and see adults in erratic and emotional behavior caused by an abusive relative or guardian. One can also drop in on our prisons and jails, and there find that over 80 percent of the inmates were convicted of crimes resulting from an antisocial behavior bred by child abuse. Children may grow out of their childhood, but because of physical or sexual abuse many do not outgrow their childhood experiences.

The loss of a child is *immeasurable*. How can a nation or a family look upon the loss of a child in the same manner as the death of a cat or dog? What is done to children ruins their lives and creates immeasurable damage that can never be repaired. No nation can suffer the loss of children and remain strong morally and in numbers. To rob a youth a place in the world is to rob that person of his inherent value. To scar a youth in childhood through abuse is to rob the youth of his potential achievements that he can use for himself, as well as the world that surrounds him. We must, as a nation and as well as families, analyze the plight of our children and effect necessary changes to assure a guaranteed life for those who someday will become the inhabitants of our world.

We must *chastise* those who think of a child as less deserving of an abuse-free life. Those who harm a child sexually, mentally, or physically must feel the weight of contempt from our society, as well as the full measure of justice from the judicial system. We need not worry about God because we recognize from His Word the condemnation facing child-haters when He calls for all of mankind to give an account before Him.

We must impose stiff sentences upon those who abuse children. We must embarrass with public disclosure and contempt the smut dealers, as well as those who buy their books, magazines, videos, and films, and attend child porno parties.

The Constitution of the United States is in all probability the greatest document mankind has ever written. It is the ultimate, in my opinion, regarding the affairs of mankind. In spite of the Constitution's magnitude, it does not supercede another great document—God's Holy Word, the Bible. The Constitution was not written to replace the Bible, but when it comes to children, it is often given precedence over God's Word. When it comes to abortion some women feel safe, relying on the principles of the Constitution. They state, "It is my Constitutional right to choose to give birth or not to give birth." They feel that the Constitution of the United States neutralizes what God has said concerning the sanctity of life, especially children, and therefore are free to do whatever they choose about their child, unborn or not.

Many in the field of pornography hide behind the First Amendment of the Constitution of the United States. They state that they can deal in child pornography legally because the Constitution of the United States allows freedom of expression and speech. They draw thousands of young people into their filthy world under the pretense that their product is protected under the Constitution.

Those who prey upon little children and scar their lives forever must be aware that God is going to judge them according to His Word, not by the liberties they sensed they had under the First Amendment of the Constitution. Those in the field of pornography should know what God has said in His Word, what He will do to those who harm kids physically, morally, or mentally.

> But whosoever shall offend one of these little ones which believe in me, it were better for him that a millstone were hanged about his neck, and that he were drowned in the depth of the sea (Matt. 18:6).

> Then were there brought unto him little children, that he should put his hands on them, and pray, and the disciples rebuked them. But Jesus said, "Suffer little children and forbid them not to come unto me: for of such is the kingdom of heaven" (Matt. 19:13,14).

Though the welfare system does a remarkable job in relieving human suffering, whether it be physically or materially, the welfare system was not created to take over the responsibility of raising and caring for one's children. Parents must realize that taking care of their children is a God-given responsibility to them, not to the government. Parents cannot escape the displeasure of a God in heaven who has stated in His Word that the parents are responsible for the welfare of the children He allows them to have.

We must *civilize* the public—*upgrading the values of a child.*

Civilize—updating modern-day attitudes towards children. There are several Biblical exhortations regarding children that the world, including America, is ignoring and neglecting concerning children and their right to live normal wholesome lives. Many of these exhortations are imbedded in the lives of biblical characters and principles.

1. The *propagation* of children (Ps. 127—128)

Lo, children are a heritage of the Lord, and the fruit of the womb is his reward. As arrows are in the hand of a mighty man, so are children of the youth. Happy is the man that hath his quiver full of them . . . (Ps. 127:3-5).

Blessed is every one that feareth the Lord; that walketh in his ways. For thou shalt eat the labor of thy hands, happy shalt thou be, and it shall be well with thee. Thy wife shall be as a fruitful vine by the sides of thine house, thy children like olive plants round about thy table (Ps. 128:1-3).

So God created man in his own image, in the image of God he created he him, male and female created he them. And God blessed them and God said unto them, Be fruitful and replenish the earth (Gen. 1:27,28).

And God blessed Noah and his sons and said unto them. Be fruitful and multiply and replenish the earth (Gen. 9:1).

Life cannot continue without reproduction: true with the animal kingdom, nature, and mankind. Each generation must replenish the land with offspring to assure that there is an abundance of life on earth. Mankind is expected to reproduce for the sake of preserving human life on earth. Today it is being said that because of the abortion era and the desire of many young adults not to have children or limit the number of children, we could very well have a shortage of human life on earth that could disrupt and even totally destroy the human race. Believe it or not, the human race is today's "endangered species." In the Western world the birth rate is declining, but in parts of the world the death rate of children is increasing to the extent that the question will be: "Where are the children?" Not "What are they doing?" but "Where are they?" It is not beyond the imagination to say, "There is no child walking in Daddy's footsteps anymore, and that is because the child no longer is alive to do so."

Should mankind produce more children than it can care for? Should there be more children than food, housing, jobs, etc.? This is a difficult question to answer and cannot be answered adequately for it brings up the fact that we need the reproduction of human life in order to preserve human life. I do not believe mankind should reduce children to the level of an animal and consider the value of a child to that of a cow or pig on a farm. A farmer will have no more livestock than he wants to manage and show a profit. I do not like "managed life-hood" and yet this is what is controlling the minds of the nations today. Perhaps that is good for China, India and other already heavily populated countries. But these countries are exceptions. Parts of the world do not have a population problem. It is my opinion that child-bearing is left up to the individual; the number of children one brings into the world is left up to his own initiative to appropriately and adequately care for. The Bible encourages reproduction and teaches that there is a blessing attached to the presence of children that cannot be surpassed by anything or person that influences a couple's life who chooses not to have children, or puts those children out of their home.

Where biblical principles are upheld, whether it be a nation or a family, children are a blessing; they are not a problem to the economy, space, or air to breath. It is my opinion that most nations with an overpopulation problem are also nations that have left God out of their lives and thus they ruin God's principles of reproduction, and their problem of overpopulation is not so much a social problem but a scriptural problem and can only be resolved by a right and true relationship with God through the Lord Jesus Christ.

2. The *pleasures* of children.

> Children's children are the crown of old men; and the
> glory of children are their fathers (Prov. 17:6).

It is sad but very true mankind today carries more credit cards in its billfolds than pictures of children. No wonder they look so sad and rejected; money cannot buy or replace the joy and comforts of children. The great center of loneliness senior citizens live in is the thought of no children to surround them. I have heard many a person say, "Instead of raising children I raised a financial empire. I wish we had taken time to raise children or I wish I had taken the same amount of time to raise my children as I took to raise my business."

When and where did we come to the place in our thinking and planning that children are a threat to our economy, happiness, and comfort?

W. A. Criswell's remark on Proverbs 17:6 is quite appropriate to our thought:

> Children are a blessing from God. How much greater
> the blessing to have a family circle consisting of chil-
> dren and grandchildren, who are as a "crown" for an
> aging patriarch. There is a delightful reciprocity here,
> for children also have "glory" in their parents through
> pride in the ancestry of a righteous father. Certainly
> there can be no greater challenge to a father than the
> admonition to live righteously in order to give his chil-
> dren reason to glory.

We live in a day where childbearing is a threat to one's personal wealth, freedom, and pleasure, whereas in days long past without children there was no wealth, freedom, or pleasure.

The Preservation of Children Without Regard to the Parents' Welfare.

There is a story written on the subject of the preservation of the child's life, whereby a parent was willing to make a great sacrifice in order to save the life of her child (1 Kings 3:16-28).

Two prostitutes had just given birth to a child. Both children were male and evidently looked very much alike. As the women slept in the same bed with the children lying beside them, one woman, having gotten up in the middle of the night, noticed that in her sleep she had rolled over on her child and accidentally smothered it to death. Quickly, while the other woman slept, she removed the live baby from his mother's side and placed the dead baby by the side of the woman who had the living baby. The mother of the dead baby then returned to bed, placing the live baby next to her. When the mother of the live baby woke up she was startled to find the dead baby by her side; she cried out, "This is not my baby, but yours," pointing to the other woman. However, the mother of the dead baby argued that the dead baby belonged to the other woman. The matter was brought before Solomon. Solomon requested that the living baby be divided in two and that each mother would receive one half of the boy's body. "Then spake the woman whose the living child was unto the king, for her bowels yearned for her son and she said, O my lord give her the living child and in no wise slay it. But the other woman said, Let it be neither mine or thine, but divide it. Then the king answered and said, Give her the living child, the woman who said ('Give the baby to her, do not kill it') and in no wise slay it: she is the mother thereof."

The hallmark of motherhood is that the child's life is

so precious that the welfare of the parents is second to the needs of the child. Somehow the attitude of the second mother prevails in our land today, an attitude that children are instruments and channels for the benefit of the parents, somehow the attitude that the child exists for the parents instead of the parents existing for the child. If an expectant mother feels that the baby she is carrying will be an embarrassment to her, or having a child will ruin her figure or will be a threat to her welfare, she might have an abortion. She does not regard the life of the child as anything more than an instrument to be used or thrown away, depending on the mother's circumstance.

The mother of Moses (Ex. 2) was faced with reporting to the Egyptian authorities that she had given birth to a boy. She knew that the boy would be slain. Rather than to see her son killed she placed him in a basket in the River Nile near the area where the daughter of Pharaoh bathed each day. Her thought was that perhaps if she could not raise the child herself, then maybe someone else would, such as Pharaoh's daughter who had no child of her own. As the baby Moses floated in the basket, the daughter of Pharaoh noticed the basket, Moses must have been crying. She commanded that the basket be brought to her. Pharaoh's daughter quickly realized what was happening. "Some Hebrew mother put the baby in the basket, hoping to save its life," she stated. Quickly she gathered the baby into her arms and decided that she would raise the boy as if it were her son. Moses' mother thought about preservation of her child, even though she would have to separate herself from him. However, Pharaoh's daughter needed a baby-sitter, and with some advice from Moses' older sister, *who just happened* to be in the presence of Pharaoh's daughter when the baby was found, recommended her mother to be the nurse and babysitter for the baby. As it turned out, Moses' mother did actually care for Moses under the roof of Pharaoh. There are ways for young mothers to care for their children; they do not have to undergo abortions in order to resolve an unwanted or unexpected pregnancy. God always has a solution for those who want to do what is right in regard to children.

The Protection of Children

There has been no child in all the world that needed more parental protection from those who would harm him than the baby Jesus. The earthly parents of Jesus displayed that parental protection, at the risk of their own lives being endangered, illustrating the care and protection modern-day children should experience from their parents or guardians.

Had Joseph taken Mary, his pregnant fiancee, to certain agencies and told them of her situation, they would have advised her to abort the child. Had Joseph taken Mary before the Pharisees they could have ordered her to be stoned, thus killing the baby Jesus. Under God's guidance Joseph protected the baby living within Mary's body. He would not allow the baby to be harmed even at the expense of his reputation and honor within his community. Both he and Mary carried the brunt of public condemnation and were willing to do so in order to allow the infant Jesus to come into the world. The birth of Jesus was a miracle, born of a virgin. However, the world knew nothing of this "birth from above" and looked upon Mary as the girl "Joseph" got into trouble. Had it not been for the strong character of Joseph and Mary it is unlikely that the baby Jesus would have survived. Parents have an obligation to protect the life that is developing in the womb regardless of how it was conceived or of what kind of a world the child will enter. Read Matthew 1:18-23.

Parental protection of one's children, without regard for themselves, is also seen in the life of the baby Jesus, when Joseph and Mary fled to Egypt to save their young child from being massacred (Matt. 2:1-14). King Herod, when hearing from the Wise Men that a king had been born, ordered the murder of all the male children under two years of age, hoping that one of them would be the child that the Wise Men had come to worship. Being warned by the angel of the Lord, Joseph and Mary left their home and business and fled to Egypt. The life and welfare of the child meant more to them than all of their possessions and position in the town. They were not willing for the child to be hurt. Even the Wise Men would not obey the king and went against his command in order to preserve and protect the young child. It is customary and expected that parents protect their children from harm, regardless of what it might cost them materially, socially, and even physically. Parents are not supposed to harm their children in any manner, and they are not to allow others to harm them either. Neighbors are expected to treat children with dignity and stay on the lookout to see that no one comes into the homes of the neighborhood and threatens the well being of the children.

Perpetuation of Personality

Children need a home to grow up in. One important value of the home is that "behind closed doors" the child is able to mature. The home is a nest where the young are taught, corrected, comforted, and challenged toward maturity. Life in the home should not stunt growth physically or mentally as well as individually. The child must be able to sense inward development that makes him realize that he is a unique individual. In homes where there is physical, mental, or sexual abuse the individuality of the person is lost and the child merely becomes a "thing" with no personal life going on inside. The biblical principles that promote and advocate the *perpetuation* of the individual personality are taught in the incident of the Lord Jesus' life when he was separated from his parents for three days while they were visiting the city of Jerusalem (Luke 2). The parents had assumed that the Lord Jesus was traveling back home with relatives. After a search through the caravan it was discovered that Jesus was not among the travelers. Mary and Joseph went back to Jerusalem and after intense searching found Him in the synagogue, surrounded by scholars, teaching the Word of God. Mary was quite upset that Jesus had caused them a delay of three days in getting back home. The Lord Jesus, at the age of twelve, answered his mother, "Know ye not that I must be about my Father's business?" The home of Joseph and Mary was a home where the Lord Jesus was given opportunity to mature toward manhood, developing His unique personality.

The home was established in order that children be brought up to become individuals, capable of leaving that home someday fully equipped physically, mentally, and spiritually to take their rightful place in the adult world. Too many of our homes produce adults in body but children mentally because of the physical and mental abuse they experience in their home life. Many of the homeless adolescents have had to leave home prematurely and thus live lives less than wholesome as adults. I have seen many adults come to the mission for help in resolving problems in their lives that should have been resolved as young children, problems such as "Who am I?" "What should I do with my life?" "How do I make a living?" etc. Too many adults are still trying to work out problems about their place in life that should have been handled while "nesting" in their homes. The Biblical principle of the home's being the place where children are allowed to be children—not bearers of pain and abuse—as well as the place where a child is given the resources to mature into a fine, healthy (mentally and physically) young adult, is predominant throughout the Holy Scriptures. There is no substitute.

We Must Mobilize

It is generally agreed that homeless children are on the increase. Yet the number is unknown, nor do we know all of the facets of life away from home these kids experience daily. As a result, there are few if any guidelines for treatment and reentry into the flow of normal life.

The Council on Scientific Affairs recommends that the American Medical Association do the following.

1. Urge that a national study providing accurate, timely, and reliable data on homeless adolescents be funded by an appropriate government agency.
2. Consider conducting a pilot study of the health care needs of homeless youths in a major city to provide physicians with solid baseline data on this issue.
3. Explore the feasibility of establishing a protocol to be used in the evaluation and treatment of homeless youth.

4. Disseminate information on the lack of treatment and health care providers for treating homeless youths.

5. Encourage state medical societies to determine the extent of treatment possible under state laws, to inform physicians of the law and regulations affecting the treatment of minors, especially those who are homeless, and to form linkages with statewide youth advocacy groups to develop protocols for the treatment of troubled youths.

6. Encourage local medical societies to develop and publicize lists of local and regional resources that can assist homeless adolescents, to provide this information to local physicians, and to establish links with providers of youth services to improve knowledge of the needs and limitations of the youths themselves and physicians who provide care.[4]

Solutions to social maladies often begin with small steps taken in local communities. The problem of throwaway children probably is no different. Though it may be impossible to get all of these youngsters off the streets, helping one or two of them need not be difficult. Persons already working on the problem have these solutions:

1. Become informed about runaway and throwaway children by writing or calling organizations that deal with these youngsters.

2. Talk to local child welfare workers. Find out what happens to homeless children in your community. Help provide the resources that are not already available.

3. Arrange for a knowledgeable speaker to address church, civic clubs, or other types of gatherings on this subject.
4. If your community lacks overnight shelter for juveniles, consider making your home available.
5. If there is a local need for a formal shelter or group home, consider working on such a project.
6. Lobby legislators to establish programs to aid these children.
7. In general, "Be involved!" says Melinda Cassidy, coordinator of volunteers for the Runaway Hotline. "Take some risks. If you know of a family with abused, neglected or troubled kids, don't look the other way."[5]

Appendix A: I'm Homeless—What Do I Do Now?

Hall

If you and/or your family are homeless, there are several avenues of help for you.

Make Connection with the Help You Need

There are more and more churches and social agencies out there to help you, but you simply need to find them. One excellent source of help is your nearest Travelers Aid. You'll find a Travelers Aid in most big American cities. In addition to locating food and shelter for you, the Travelers Aid social worker can put you in touch with other services you may need for yourself and your family.

Some Travelers Aid branches directly provide services you need while others assist you with the means to get to other sources of help. If there is no Travelers Aid in your city, call the United Way for information and referral to the local organization that has been established to help you while you are homeless.

If you seek a church for help, accept whatever help it offers and also ask the church to connect you with the local source of emergency food and shelter.

Go from a Crisis to Stability

Once you have found emergency help for yourself and your family, start planning for your future. You must devise a *plan* that will move you from your homeless situation and into a place of your own. Help with this plan can be forthcoming from several sources: Travelers Aid (if that's where you started); another social-service agency that works with homeless individuals and families; some churches which have this service; some missions and shelters who have counselors to help you. If you can't locate the kind of help you need, ask for it. This plan is too important "just to happen." *You have to make it happen.*

If you are unemployed, your plan should include how to find and keep a job. There are programs available that will (1) help you work on your skills so you will have something to offer a prospective employer; (2) help you learn how to handle job interviews so you can present yourself in the best possible light; (3) enable you to have clean, presentable clothes for that job interview; and (4) assist you in working on problems which have interfered with your ability to get or keep a job.

If you are using *drugs and/or alcohol,* you *absolutely must* get help to overcome these problems. Even though many drug/alcohol treatment programs have waiting lists, it is vital that you receive the necessary treatment, *no matter how long it takes.* Having an advocate, an advisor-friend who will get you on the list and will help you to make it while you're waiting, is important. Look for such an advocate at the organizations which have helped you.

No matter what your situation is, *keep your children in school.* Whether it's a classroom in a shelter or being bused to a school across town, education is a serious key to your children's future. They must not miss out on this door-opener! Do your best to help them feel good about themselves, even though all of you are homeless. If they have you, your love, and your support, your children will be able to handle a period of homelessness.

The best boost you can give them is to make definite plans for leaving this homeless situation for a stable homelife.

Never overlook the power of God in helping you to develop and follow through on your plan to escape homelessness. Bible reading, prayer, and worship are powerful forces in overcoming those problems which have stood in your pathway. Many of our most effective treatment programs recognize and use the power of God in overcoming addiction problems.

And look to God's people to help you. Many churches around this country are responding to the problem of homelessness through numerous approaches and programs. They are often providing food and shelter, assisting homeless persons with funds to reach help in another area, providing counseling, support, and love, as well as other kinds of help. Churches are a good source of information about what else is available in the community.

Above all, *hold on to hope!* By taking the steps above and developing a plan to move you and your family out of homelessness, you have a reason to be hopeful. Using all your own resources as well as those of the community, the churches, and any other entitlements for which you qualify, you have created a formula for success. *You can make it!*

Appendix B: Who Can Help the Runaway?

Resener

"You never get the same kid back after the first runaway experience," Diane Flannery of San Francisco's Larkin Street Youth Shelter says.

> The streets are so addictive it's hard to go back to anything else. There are no rules, no school, just a big party at first. And after living with the freedom to come and go it's tough to return to a family with curfews and rules. If they stay awhile the streets mark kids permanently. It is nearly impossible to integrate back into school after working as a prostitute for three years. We try very hard to get to kids before they run away or as soon as they hit the streets. It is their best chance.[1]

What are the chances that a young runaway can be reached and led away from the streets before they get lost in the runaway syndrome? So many young people who live on the streets do not know of the organizations they can look to for help. There are over 300 runaway outreach programs in the country, offering a variety of services ranging from food and shelter to long-term sheltering.

The following is the list of organizations that can assist young runaways.

Boston

The Bridge Over Troubled Waters, Boston, MA. 617/ 423-9575.

Calhoun, TN
Shenandoah Ranch, 615/336-3835.

Chattanooga, TN
Teen Challenge, 615/756-5558 (107 centers throughout the nation).

Chicago
Neon Street Center, Chicago, IL. 312/528-7767.

Evansville, IN
Evansville Rescue Mission, 812/421-3800.

Hillsborough, NH
His Mansion, 607/243-8126.

Indianapolis, IN
Wheeler Rescue Mission, 317/635-3575.

Kansas City
Neutral Ground, Kansas City, KS. 913/342-5121.
City Union Mission, 816/474-9380.

Lakemont, NY
Freedom Village, 607/243-8126.

Los Angeles
Children of the Night, Los Angeles, CA. 213/461-3160.
Youth With a Mission, P.O. Box 1110, Hollywood, CA 90078. 213/463-5433.

Miami
The Bridge, 1149 N.W. 11th St., Miami, FL 33136. 305/324-8953.

Appendix B: Who Can Help the Runaway?

Nashville

Nashville Union Rescue Mission, Anchor Home-Young Men 17-23, 615/255-2475 or 615/244-8178.

Oasis Center, 1216 17th Ave., S., Nashville, TN 37203. 615/320-0026.

Portland

The Salvation Army Greenhouse, 820 S.W. Oak, Portland, OR 97208. 503/223-2997.

San Jose, CA

City Team Ministries, 408/998-4770.

San Francisco

Larkin Street Youth Shelter, 1044 Larkin St., San Francisco, CA 94109. 401/673-0911.

Seattle

New Horizons, P.O. Box 2801, 1406 Summit Ave., Seattle, WA 98122. 206/328-0155.

Union Gospel Mission of Seattle, 206/723-0767.

Syracuse, NY

Rescue Mission Alliance, Inc. 315/476-7941.

National

National Network of Runaway and Youth Services, 1400 I Street N.W., Washington, D.C. 20005. 202/682-4114.

Child Help USA (Child Abuse Hotline)

1-800-422-4453. Crisis counseling for abused youth and for parents involved in child abuse situations; referrals to local programs and help in reporting abuse to state agencies.

National Council on Child Abuse and Domestic Violence

1-800-222-2000 (in California 1-818-914-2814). Information on child abuse and other types of family violence.

Parents Anonymous

1-800-421-0353 (in California, 1-800-352-0386). Referrals to local self-help groups for abusive parents or those who fear they will do so.

Domestic Violence Shelter Aid Hotline

1-800-333-SAFE. Referrals for victims of domestic violence.

Missing Youth National Center for Missing and Exploited Youth

1-800-843-5678 (in Washington, D.C., 634-9836). A clearinghouse for information on missing and exploited youth; helps parents locate missing children; distributes photos and descriptions; and provides assistance to law enforcement.

Child Find of America, Inc.

1-800-426-5678. Assistance in locating missing children; national photo distribution and registration; information on prevention; helps parents returning from hiding with abducted children.

Alcohol Hotline/Alcoholics Anonymous/Alanon/Alateen

1-800-ALCOHOL. Referrals to local support groups for alcoholics, families of alcoholics and teens who have parents or siblings with a drinking problem. Referrals for those needing alcohol counseling.

Cocaine Hotline

1-800-COCAINE. Information and referrals on drug abuse, not only cocaine.

National Institute on Drug Abuse

1-800-662-HELP. Crisis counseling for substance abusers and referrals for treatment.

Pride Drug Information Line

1-800-241-9746. Information on substance abuse and referrals to local programs.

AIDS Hotline

(U.S. Public Health Service), 1-800-342-AIDS. Information on AIDS and referrals for testing and counseling.

STD Hotline

1-800-227-8922. Information on sexually transmitted diseases and referrals for testing and treatment.

Birthright

1-800-848-5683 (in New Jersey, 1-609-848-1819). Referrals to local Birthright organizations which will assist pregnant women of all ages with support and counseling.

Travelers Aid is located in most every major city in the U.S.

Resener

"Fix the Kid!"

I remember the startling reality of an outraged father of a runaway, when I called to let him know his son was staying at the Nashville Union Mission. His reply was, "I sure hope you can do something for him. We sure as ___ couldn't." As I have visited several shelters around the country I have discovered that workers at the shelters have heard the same caustic remarks. One such shelter director summed it up: "Many parents hope their runaway will meet some responsible person who will turn their child into a 'nice, sweet, obedient person.'" In my opinion, many parents believe that running away would be the best thing for their child if it meant the child would end up somewhere he could be helped to "correct his behavior."

If the runaway child is fortunate enough to find his way to one of many youth shelters available to him, there could be some positive influences at a shelter.

The kid will be protected. All of the runaway shelters Dr. Hall and I have visited are headed up by conscientious workers, dedicated to the welfare of the kid. Once inside the door of the shelter the runaway will be protected from the physical and mental harm prevalent on the streets.

The kid will be provided for. If a young person has been on the streets any length of time he will probably eat his first decent meal at a youth shelter. Many of the runaways I have seen in youth shelters, across the country, are far from hunger. Though many show the signs of being without consistent, balanced meals, they do reveal that they have access to sufficient food. Medical assistance, including dental care, is also available to the residents.

Since the runaway left most of his clothing at home, he soon needs new or at least clean clothing. This is readily available in most youth shelters. The style may not be fashionable, but at least the clothing articles are free of charge and fitting for the season.

The kid is encouraged. Most of the runaways or castaways are in a state of deep depression and discouragement over what happened to them at home and over what they have experienced while on the streets. The purpose of the youth shelter is not only to keep a kid from self-destruction, but to help him have some self-esteem about himself. Many a homeless kid experiences self-worth, buoyed by a worker in the local youth shelter. It is easy to feel bad about oneself after leaving home and living on the streets. At such a crucial time, a youth shelter can play a vital role in whether the kid continues his journey to nowhere or will accept the help of the youth shelter personnel and begin to reevaluate his life. Pimps, drug pushers, and porn peddlers do all they can to discredit youth shelters. Those leeches are well aware shelters can give the runaway an opportunity to break away from their grasp. Our shelter here in Nashville has been the object of harassment, ridicule, and slander by those who were losing money from the young lives that had sought the young men's home for refuge and direction in life. Belief in one's self, trust in others and God—especially in the religious youth centers—are focal points in motivating a young person to rethink his life's plan and to seek help enabling him to establish a beneficial life-style and behavior.

The kid is prepared. Many youth shelters across the nation offer educational programs for homeless kids. Many young persons failed to finish their education, making it almost impossible for them to land a suitable job. This is one reason why many kids turn to crime-drugs-sex. However, at a qualified youth shelter one can complete his education which may well help him obtain a suitable, decent job that will provide him financial assistance. We have personally seen virtual miracles at the classes provided by the Nashville Union Mission.

I speak from my own situation and calling. The religious-based youth shelter not only can help a young person learn to make a living but to know how to live as well. The religious-based youth centers seek to establish a living relationship between the runaway and God. Oftentimes spiritual problems created the issue that caused the kid to leave home. Many young persons who accepted the Lord's helping hand while residing at our young men's home are today successful businessmen and church leaders, as well as heads of Christian homes.

The kid will be loved. One would think that a youth shelter for runaways and castaways would resemble a youth-detention center or boot camp for young marines. However, I have found most youth shelters across the nation to be centers of love, affection, and genuine concern for street kids. Street kids often look on the personnel of the shelter as substitute moms and dads. The fact that the shelter workers want to help a wandering, floundering young person has a tremendous impact on a kid who finds it difficult to trust a soul with his or her innermost feelings. One of the runaway's biggest mistakes—and probably the overriding reason why he is reluctant to enter a shelter—is that he prejudges a shelter worker to be at the shelter for selfish motives. I have often seen young men completely break down and cry in the arms of a counselor upon discovering that the worker was really interested in their welfare. Young people must eventually leave a shelter. In most cases they walk away in the middle of the day, saying good-bye with tears and handshakes, quite the opposite when they fled, in the darkness of the night, from their homes.

In spite of the quality work accomplished in youth centers there are several things the centers cannot provide. The shelter workers should not be under the pressure of "fixing up the kid," primarily due to the fact that the kid's "life was shattered at home," and if there is "fixing" to do, then the home must also require "fixing."

Youth shelters cannot *remove scars* of the past, physically, mentally, or socially. Oftentimes parents of street kids want the shelter worker to be a spokesperson for them in hopes of encouraging the kid to return home. The hurt the young person may have experienced at home is often so deep that he/she has no desire to return home and will not listen to the advice of the shelter worker. A youth shelter may be able to remove the terror of being on the streets but can do little to dispel the horror that was generated by continued incidents of physical and mental abuse perpetuated by the parents and relatives of the runaway.

Youth shelters cannot *rebuild the past*. Youth shelters can build highways for the future but are not able to rebuild bridges of the past. It is not unusual for a shelter worker to be asked by a parent of a runaway, "Please get my son or daughter to love me again." Youth shelters do help runaways and castaways return home; however, the binding of the wounds created by the home situations depends entirely upon the parents and the young person. The problems of guilt, fear, resentment, and even suicide are dealt with by concerned and conscientious workers in the shelters. Most street kids tell me that the youth shelter is a good place to go, because the workers are willing to listen to their side of the story. Shelters can help prepare a disturbed and disoriented young person to face his past but can do little about expunging the past to the extent that the parent(s) and young person can live in harmony. Rebuilding the past must involve both the parent and the young person. Parents should not expect that shelter or other services to do it all.

Youth centers cannot *remake lives*. Youth shelters can only *repair* broken lives. Reverend Leonard Nabors, supervisor of our young men's program, recalls the question of a young man's parents. Before coming to the shelter, he had been living on the streets and had developed a cocaine addiction. Their query to Nabors, having learned that their son was a resident of the shelter, was, "How long will it take you to get our son straight?" It is strange but true a parent can have a young person for sixteen-seventeen years under his guidance, see the child rebel and leave home, and when he discovers his offspring is in a shelter, the question arises, "How long will it take for you to fix him up so he can return home?" Parents actually believe shelters can do in weeks what all those years did not do in the life of the runaway. Youth centers cannot *replace homes*. Parents who are content with others fulfilling their responsibility are abdicating a titanic priority.

Youth shelters are not homes in structure or in authority. The director of a shelter should not and cannot replace the father's and mother's role. The house mother cannot fill the role of the mother, although in most shelters, she is considered "Mom" by the residents.

Kids in a shelter must have more than the help of the shelter workers to set goals and principles for their lives. This is the role only parents can fill, and they should be jealous of others who are fulfilling those tasks. Parents must not feel content that their runaway child is in a shelter; that is not where they belong, and parents should be willing to "fix up the home" so that their child will go home.

What will it require to "fix the kid"—if not the shelters, then what and who are capable of handling this monumental onus?

Parents of a runaway must realize that "fixing up the kid" does not involve his life away from home as much as it involves his life, as it was, at home. The problems—and they can be many and extremely complicated—that the runaway experiences while he is on the streets can in due time be overcome after the runaway leaves the street. What continues, however, and must be resolved are the problems that triggered the running-away episode.

The father of the "prodigal son" met the boy with an open *head*. We do not know how long the boy had been away from home; we do know, though, that the father spotted his ragged, worn-out son approaching him. The boy made the first step at reconciliation by coming home to face however the father responded to his presence. Then it was up to the father if the boy kept on going past the farm or walked through the gate and into the arms of his father. The father ran to the frail boy and put his arms around him. Instead of bargaining with or branding the boy with the terms of his readmittance into the family circle, the father dominated the scene with understanding and sensibility, as well as with reasonable utterances that caused the boy to feel he made the right choice in returning home. So many young people who run away believe there will be no one waiting at the door to let a bewildered runaway in.

The father met the boy with an *open heart*. The boy

had his speech memorized. However, before he could confess he had done wrong, the father was consoling him, telling him, "It's going to be all right." I imagine that the first few minutes were spent with both confessing wrong deeds that initiated the boy's departure. I can hear the father saying to the boy, "Son, I'm sorry I didn't take the time to see if everything was OK with you. I just got too busy with the farm duties that I ignored you. Son, I am sorry."

I can also hear the boy reply, "Dad, I'm sorry I was so impatient with you. I thought life on the farm was lived in the 'slow lane.' I shouldn't have left you as I did." The dad could have cursed the boy. He could have said, "Son, you keep on moving. I do not have a place in my heart for you. I cried my last tear for you the day you left." The father, however, met the boy with an open heart of love and affection. He felt, "I don't care where he's been, how long he's been gone. He's home now, he's safe, and I am so happy!"

The father met the runaway with an *open hand.* "Spent all you had? Your money all gone on foolishness?" The father could have greeted his boy with these cruel—and perhaps justifiable—remarks. The father instructed servants, "Get him some clothes, sandals, and put some T-bone steaks on the grill. We are going to have a welcome-home party." The father could have closed his home to the boy, but instead he made available all he possessed to the boy. The father did not use the runaway boy's appearance as a means of judgment or criticism. He simply requested that the dirty, torn clothes be replaced by better ones. It would have been cruel, as well as useless, to make an issue of what was quite obvious to the boy—that he needed a new wardrobe. I am sure what the father did not say was as meaningful as what he did say to his son. Isn't that what love is all about?

The father met the boy with an *open home*. Arriving home the boy was greeted with love and understanding; he was fed and clothed from the father's resources. There was one more symbol to be expressed, and that was accomplished when the father placed the family ring on his hand. This act meant that he was once more a member of the family, without probation or a trial period. The father received his son back into the family, as well as in his heart. One wonders if the father's heart ever was closed to the boy, but only the father could have revealed it. There are many youth on the streets who would run home if they thought there ever was a slim chance to be received as the prodigal son was, restored into the family structure. In many situations involving a runaway the best "fix-it program" is in the hands of the parents of the runaway.

When the Civil War was over, men asked President Abraham Lincoln how he would treat the Southern states, who left the Republic. President Lincoln replied, "We will treat them as if they never left!" Parents would do well if they practiced the same gracious philosophy.

Notes

Chapter 1

1. *Youth Worker,* Winter, 1989, 67-69.
2. *Newsweek,* April 25, 1988, 64.
3. *Home Life,* June 1980, 6.
4. *US New and World Report,* November 7, 1988, 34ff.
5. Penelope L. Maza and Judy A. Hall, *Homeless Children and Their Families: A Preliminary Study* (New York: Child Welfare League of America, 1988).

Chapter 2

1. Jan Read, "Homeless Children Need Special Help, Educators Say," *Nashville Banner,* February 7, 1989.

Chapter 3

1. Claudia Levy, "Maryland's Homeless Increasingly Moderate-income Families," *Washington (D.C.) Post,* April 10, 1989.
2. Fred Grimm, *No Time for Fairy Tales* (Nashville: Impact Books, 1980).

Chapter 4

1. Ellen L. Bassuk, L. Rubin, and A. S. Lauriat, "Characteristics of Sheltered Homeless Families," *American Journal of Public Health,* September; 1986, 76(9), 1097-1101.
2. W. A. Criswell, *With a Bible in My Hand* (Nashville: Broadman Press, 1978), 24-25.

Chapter 5

1. Jim Hubbard, free-lance writer and photographer in Takoma Park, Maryland, *Signs of the Times,* 2-1989, 12.
2. *Newsweek,* Ibid.
3. *Youth Worker,* Winter 1989, 67.
4. *Youth Worker,* Ibid.

Chapter 6

1. Brian L. Harbour, *From Cover to Cover* (Nashville: Broadman Press, 1982), 118.
2. Ibid.
3. Lyle Schaller, *Understanding Tomorrow* (Nashville: Abingdon Press, n. d.), 46-49.
4. Harbour, Ibid., 119-120.

Chapter 8

1. Ahmad Ardekani, *The Protector*, May-June, 1989, 12A.

Chapter 9

1. *Newsweek*, Ibid.
2. Herb Pfiffer, *You Can Have Tremendous Kids*, July-September, 1988.

Chapter 10

1. Charles H. Spurgeon, *Metropolitan Tabernacle Pulpit* (Pasadena, TX: Pilgrim Publications, 1971), 692.
2. Barbara Baumgardner, "When Our Children Disappoint Us," *Decision*, October 1988, 16-17.

Epilogue

1. John Bishop Peale. Quoted by P. Hallie. *Lest Innocent Blood Be Shed* (New York: Harper & Row, 1979), 2784. *JAMA*, September 8, 1989, Vol. 262, No. 10, 1376.
2. *Kiwanis* Magazine, November-December 1988, 31.
3. Jesse Jackson, *Modern Maturity*, August-September 1989, 35.
4. *The Journal of the American Medical Association*, Vol. 262, No. 10, Sept. 8, 1989, 1361.
5. *Kiwanis*, November-December 1988, 33.

Appendix B

1. *Youth Worker*, Ibid.

Bibliography

Adams, Gerald R., Gullotta, Thomas, Clancy, Mary Anne. "Homeless Adolescents: A Descriptive Study of Similarities and Differences between Runaways and Throwaways," *Adolescence*, Fall 1985, Vol. XX, No. 79, 715-724.

Ardekani, Ahmad. *The Protector*, May-June, 1989, 12A.

Batchelor, Dick J. *Orlando Sentinel*, 1988.

Bassuk, Ellen L., Rubin, L., and Lauriat, A. S. "Characteristics of Sheltered Homeless Families." *American Journal of Public Health*, 1986, September 76 (9), 1097-1101.

Baumgardner, Barbara, "When our Children Disappoint Us," *Decision*, October 1988, 16-17.

Chea, Alvin and Anthony Jones. *Message, Child Abuse*, April 1989.

"Facts for Families," *The American Academy of Child and Adolescent Psychiatry*. Vol. I, No. 10.

Gewirtzman, R. and Rodor, I. "The Homeless Child at School: From Welfare Hotel to Classroom," *Child Welfare*, May-June 1987, 66(3), 237-45.

Grimm, Fred. *No Time for Fairy Tales*. (Nashville: Impact Books, 1980).

Hagen, J. "Gender and Homelessness," *Social Work*, 1987, 312-16.

Hallie, P. "Lest Innocent Blood Be Shed," *JAMA*, September 8, 1989, Vol. 262, No. 10, 1376.

Harbour, Brian J. *From Cover to Cover* (Nashville: Broadman Press, 1982).

Hiratsuka, Jon. "Homeless Kids Face Barrier to Schooling," *NASW News*, March, 1989.

Homelessness: Critical Issues for Policy and Practice,
The Boston Foundation, 1987.

Home Life, June 1980, 6.

Hubbard, Jim. Freelance writer and photographer in Takoma Park, Maryland, *Signs of the Times,* February,
1989, 12.

Institute of Medicine—Committee on Health Care for
Homeless People. *Homelessness, Health, and Human Needs* (National Academy Press 1988).

Jennings, Lisa. "Report Expected to Sharpen Policy De-
bate on Homeless," *Education Week,* February 8,
1989, Volume VIII, Number 20.

Joint Center for Housing Studies of Harvard University.
The State of the Nation's Housing 1988 (Cambridge,
Massachusetts, 1988.

The Journal of the American Medical Association.
Vol. 262, No. 10, September 8, 1989.

Kaufman, Nancy K. "Help for the Homeless: The Massachusetts Experience," *Harvard Public Policy Review,*
Spring, 1989, 3-11.

Kesler, Jay, General Editor. *Parents and Teenagers* (Vic-
tor Books 1984).

Kurtz, Howard. "For Homeless N.Y. Children, Mobile
Unit Is What Doctor Ordered," *Washington Post,*
March 21, 1989.

Kurtz, Howard. "Welfare Hotel Occupants at Eye of Po-
litical Storm in New York." *Washington Post,* A3,
September 15, 1987.

Kyle, John E., Editor. *Children, Families & Cities,* December 1987.

Levy, Claudia. "Maryland's Homeless Increasingly
Moderate-Income Families," *Washington Post,* April
18, 1989.

Likhavov, Albert. Soviets Children's Foundation, 1987.

Manuel, Patricia Pastan. *Sheltering Homeless Women.* Doctoral Dissertation, Boston University, 1986.

Maza, Penelope L. and Hall, Judy A. *Homeless Children and Their Families: A Preliminary Study.* Child Welfare League of America: 1988.

McCall, Ella. "I Tell Homeless Kids, 'Love You, Baby,'" *New York Times,* November, 1, 1988.

McChesney, Kay Young, *Women Without: Homeless Mothers and Their Children.* Doctoral Dissertation, University of Southern California, 1987.

Melnick, V. L., and Williams, D. S. "Children and Families Without Homes: Observations from Thirty Case Studies," *Homelessness in the District of Columbia.* (Center for Applied Research and Urban Policy. UDC, 1987.)

Molnar, Janice, Klein, Tovah, Knitzer, Jane and Ortiz-Torres, Blanca. *Home Is Where the Heart Is: The Crisis of Homeless Children and Families in New York City,* Bank Street College of Education, March, 1988.

Nashville Tennessean, May 7, 1989.

Newsweek, April 25, 1988, 64-68.

New York State Department of Social Services. *No Time to Lose,* 1988.

Nichols, J., Wright, L. K., and Murphy, J. F. "A Proposal for Tracking Health Care for the Homeless," *Journal of Community Health.* 1986, 11(3); 204-09.

Pfiffer, Herb. *You Can Have Tremendous Kids,* Rescue publication, July-September, 1988.

Pinellas County Coalition for the Homeless. *Winter 1988 Homeless Survey.* May 1988.

Read, Jan. "Homeless Children Need Special Help, Educators Say," *Nashville Banner,* February 7, 1989.

Robertson, Julia. (May, 1988) "Homeless Adolescents A Hidden Population," *Hospital and Community Psychiatry* as described in June 1988 *Children & Teens Today*, 7.

Rosa, Alfredo de la. (January, 1989). "Heritage Foundation Examines Homelessness," *American Family*, vol. 12, no. 1, 21.

Rosenman, Mark and Stein, Mary Lee. *Homeless Children: A New Vulnerability*, October 1987.

Russo, Tony, Consortium for Services to Homeless Families, Washington, D.C.

Sanchez, Rene. "For Homeless, School No Shelter from Shame," *Washington Post*, December 19, 1988.

Schwartz, Rita. *The Impact of the Homeless on the Transformation Industry*, 1988.

Settje, Lisa. *Reader's Digest*, June, 1989, 128.

Spolar, Chris. (May 29, 1989) "Homelessness Frustrates District's Best Efforts," *Washington Post*.

Spurgeon, Charles H. (1971) *Metropolitan Tabernacle Pulpit*, vol. 21 (Pilgrim Publications: Pasadena, TX), 692.

Street World. (New York: Street World, 1989).

Taylor, Martien. "Homelessness: The Nature of the Crisis," *Housing*, June, 1988, 5-7.

Texas Health and Human Services Coordinating Council. *Final Report on the Homeless in Texas*. October 1985.

The National Alliance to End Homelessness. *Housing and Homelessness*, June 1988.

U.S. News & World Report. November 7, 1988, 34-40.

United States Conference of Mayors. *The Continuing Growth of Hunger, Homelessness, and Poverty in*

America's Cities: 1978. A 26-City Survey, 1987.

United States Conference of Mayors. *A Status Report on Hunger and Homelessness in America's Cities: 1988,* January 1989.

United States Department of Education. *News,* February 17, 1989.

Wasem, Ruth Ellen. (March 17, 1989). "Homelessness: Issues and Legislation in the 101st Congress," *CRS Issue Brief.*

Whitman, David, "Shattering Myths about the Homeless," *U.S. News & World Report,* March 20, 1989.

Youth Worker. Winter 1989, 67-69.

About the Authors

DR. CARL R. RESENER and DR. JUDY HALL are two outstanding advocates for the homeless in America. They bring together a total of sixty-four years serving in the area of social work and ministries.

The Rev. Dr. Resener has been executive director of the Nashville Union Mission since 1971. Previously, he had worked at the Mission from 1957-1961 and as a pastor from 1962-1970. Resener has studied at Purdue University, Bob Jones University (B.A., B.D.), the universities of Georgia, Nebraska, Washington in St. Louis, Memphis State, Harvard, and Volunteer State College. Heritage Baptist University (Indianapolis) honored him with the D.D. He has published two books, *Crisis in the Streets* (Broadman, 1988) and *Taking the Alcoholic out of Alcoholism.*

Under his leadership the Union Mission has ministries to young men and women, a drug and alcohol rehab center, care for families, a women's and children's center, educational and vocational school availability, a men's division, Travelers Aid, and medical and dental facilities.

Dr. Judy Hall is an author and social worker who has related extensively to families and children. Since 1986 she has been a senior social work executive at the national level in both Travelers Aid International and the National Association of Social Workers where she has conducted research into the multiple causes of homelessness among children and families.

She has a B.A. and an M.S.W. from Washington University in St. Louis and a Ph.D. from St. Louis University. She has done additional graduate work at Rollins College, Webster College, and the universities of Nebraska and Missouri. She has written and spoken extensively on the subject of homelessness.